Posing and Solving Problems
with Story Boxes

1st & 2nd Grade

Donna Burk
San Jose, California
a graduate of the University of Oregon
a primary classroom teacher

Allyn Snider
Portland, Oregon
a graduate of the University of Oregon
a primary classroom teacher

QPS172   SB12-1
POS807   08140

Published by The Math Learning Center, Salem, Oregon

Posing and Solving Problems with Story Boxes
1st and 2nd Grades
Includes a set of blackline masters, packaged separately

Library of Congress Catalog Card Number: 94-075180

P0602
Prepared for publication on Macintosh Desktop Publishing system.

Printed in the United States of America

ISBN 1-886131-25-2

This book is dedicated to

— the children who teach us.

— hard working, dedicated teachers
who attend our workshops and challenge us.

— The Math Learning Center and Toby Gordon of
Heinemann Books for their faith and trust.

Acknowledgements

We give many thanks to:

Paula Symonds,
San Francisco, California,
for her support;

The children of
Wilsonville Primary School,
Wilsonville, Oregon, and
George Miner School,
San Jose, California,
for teaching us;

Sharon LeBlond, Oxford, Maine,
Peggy Steinbronn, Des Moines, Iowa,
Tom Antang, San Jose, California,
for invaluable feedback, friendship,
and support;

Jill Ostrow, Wilsonville, Oregon,
for her unbelievable energy and
willingness to trade story problems
back and forth;

Chris Waller,
Oak Grove School District,
San Jose, California,
Marilyn Seger, West Linn-Wilsonville
School District, Wilsonville, Oregon,
for being very insightful observers of
classroom life;

Dr. Michael Arcidiacono,
Portland State University,
Portland, Oregon,
for reading, contributing suggestions,
and offering mathematical
advice;

Dr. Rosemary Wray Williams,
Lewis and Clark College,
Lake Oswego, Oregon,
for contributing insights about life,
learning, teaching, and
assessment;

Marilyn Burns, Kathy Richardson,
and the late Mary Baratta-Lorton,
for inspiration;

our families,
for their incredible patience and
loving support.

Artists and Designers:
Gayle Steinberger, Paula Ogi, Ryan
Wilkerson, Jonathan Maier, Sue
Schlichting, Vaunie Maier, and our
students.

Contents

Preface

B ack in the mid-1980's, we developed a set of materials based on Mary Baratta-Lorton's *Workjobs*, called Story Boxes. In this collection, there were eighteen boxes, each containing eight picture boards and seventy to eighty small counters to be used in conjunction with the boards. There were such scenes as meadows with butterfly counters, ponds with miniature frogs, beaches with tiny shells, and fields with lima bean lady bugs. Our idea was that children could come to understand the processes of counting, adding, and subtracting, as well as how these processes were symbolized, by moving counters around their boards in response to such stories as:

"The little girl collected seven shiny shells. Can you show the shells she collected on your board?"

"Five frogs were playing in the pond. Four more came to join them. How many in all?"

"I made eight valentines and put three into the mailbox. How many do I have left to deliver?"

"The wildlife biologist thought she'd seen six jungle birds in the tree, but when she looked again, she only saw two. How many had flown away?"

We intended that children would also tell, and eventually write, their own story problems, using the counters and boards to prompt language that might otherwise be difficult. We used the Story Boxes extensively in our own classrooms and included them in our teachers' guides and seminars. Teachers frequently chose to make them during workshops, but sometimes found they weren't sure how to use them back in their classrooms.

In the summer of 1992 we decided to write a more comprehensive guide to the Story Boxes, incorporating some of the changes mandated by the new NCTM Curriculum Standards, and attempting to use the materials in more open-ended ways ourselves. Was there a way, we wondered, to move beyond simple addition and subtraction situations to more complex problems? Could young children be expected to deal with the dynamics of missing addends, missing subtrahends, differencing, partitioning, multiplication, and division? Was there a way to move from rote practice to problem solving at a level appropriate to our first and second graders? Was it possible, furthermore, to help our students learn to pose, as well as solve, interesting and challenging problems?

We made several discoveries early that fall in our own classrooms. The first was that children enjoyed trying to solve challenging problems. Although we were sure to "lose" some of our students along the way, we saw a higher level of interest when the problems we posed required some real thinking. Many youngsters were intrigued by problems that required operations they hadn't been taught. When we showed them fourteen glowing eyes and asked them to figure out how many pumpkins were in the window, the fact that they didn't know how to "do division" was not an issue. Some counted by twos or set out pumpkin counters on their boards until they could see fourteen eyes, while others simply looked on, knowing it was okay to watch. A few reached a solution by adding two sevens or "just knowing" there were seven twos in fourteen.

We also found that at first children were able to solve much more challenging problems than they could pose. In fact, writing and reading story problems early in the year turned out to be so difficult for many of our first graders that we had to devise some common picture formats they could use. Pictures in conjunction with numbers and a few simple words created settings, and strategically placed question marks signaled the problems to be solved. (See Neal's story problem on following page.)

Second graders were capable of writing simple story problems from the beginning, but we found that many of them needed to create pictures first to clarify their own thinking about situations more complex than basic addition and subtraction.

First and second graders alike relied on our models and ideas at first, copying or modifying them only slightly. As the year progressed, some began to devise their own problems or add unique twists to ours. JoDell took the

Neal

The Stor whnts 10 Baers
HoW many myeodo
they need

The store wants ten bears. How many do they need?
by Neal

multiplication model we offered in October and made it just a step harder:

There were 8 windows in the haunted house, and three pumpkins in each window. How many *eyes* altogether?

Michael, along with many others, used large numbers to make his problems more challenging.

There were 35 crates. How many teddy bears? (Each crate holds 5 bears.)

Sara discovered that she could make her classmates think by choosing her numbers very carefully:

One day the Teddy Bear Store had 25 bears. A mom walked in and said, "I need 25 bears and I have 8 children. But I don't know how many they each get."

Mike increased the level of complexity by writing a problem with more than one solution:

I went to the bear store. I had seventeen dollars. How many bears could I buy? (All the brown bears cost $5.00 each, and all the tan bears cost $4.00 each.)

As the school year progressed, we began to appreciate the power of story problems, both as a tool to promote understanding of basic operations and number sense, and as a way to encourage mathematical communication between students. Children were greatly motivated to create problems that would challenge their classmates. However, it took time for some of them to understand that the object was to pose *workable* problems. By mid-year, some second graders were even able to help one another revise their initial problems, asking "I don't understand what you want me to do here—can you make the problem more clear?" "Can we make it so hard that even Tessia can't do it?"

Throughout the year, students worked on one another's problems together, enacting them with storyboards and counters. They explained their ideas and solutions verbally and sometimes demonstrated their thinking at the overhead. Our focus was process- rather than product-oriented ("How did you figure that out? Did anyone have a different way? We have quite a variety of answers here—do all of them work?"), and through our discussions we tried to capitalize on children's errors and misconceptions. We also encouraged children to set their thinking down on paper; to communicate how they'd arrived at their solutions by means of sketches, numbers, and/or words. Exchanging story problems with children from other classes in the spring provided our second graders with even more motivation to communicate their thinking clearly in written form.

Eventually, story problems became a filter children used to process events in the classroom and at home. Crackers were set out for snack—how many more did you get than me? We wanted to make juice for a party—how many cans of mix would we have to buy, and how much would it cost? There were seven planting boxes for our seeds. How many more would we need? As teachers, we learned to live with the fact that not every child was able to solve or even understand every problem we posed, nor could they always work their classmates' problems. It seemed that in the process of trying to pose and solve story problems all year, however, all of our students became comfortable with a range of operations, gained number sense, and grew as mathematical risk-takers. We are excited to share our new work with you, and hope you find it valuable in your own classroom.

Introduction

"Problem solving is not a distinct topic, but a process which should permeate the entire program and provide the context in which concepts and skills can be learned."

National Council of Teachers of Mathematics

"It is through open discussion that mathematical understanding is developed, concepts are formed, and the appropriate mathematical vocabulary and language structures are practiced and modeled. It is through language that students make meaning of their mathematical experiences and develop confidence in what they have learned."

Rex Stoessiger and Joy Edmunds, *Natural Learning and Mathematics*

Many of us who are teachers have come to accept the idea that reading can't really be "taught". We can read to children and share big books. As experienced users of print, we can model such strategies as moving our eyes from left to right, pointing to individual words as we recite familiar text, using context clues in conjunction with initial consonants to predict unfamiliar words, and skipping words we just can't get. We can surround our students with print and share our own love of literature. Many of us believe that in the end, children must sort reading out for themselves, in much the same way they learn language.

Why, then, is it so difficult to trust that learning mathematics might work the same way? Is it because math seems so logical, so sequential? Mustn't children learn to add before they subtract and multiply before they divide? Shouldn't these skills be carefully taught? We know if we offer children enough opportunities to read and write, most of them will learn how. But what's the equivalent in mathematics?

We can imagine a roomful of children writing, using whatever skills they have at the time to communicate their ideas; story telling and invented spelling are wonderful tools for beginning readers, but how does one use successive approximation in math when there's usually only one right answer? We know how to create print-rich environments in our classrooms, but is there such a thing as a mathematics-rich environment. If so, what does it look like? If whole meaningful texts and real reasons to write propel language learning, what is the mathematical parallel?

Over the past year, we have discovered that story problems based on such familiar themes as riding the school bus, giving and receiving presents, and shopping can provide challenges for children to tackle in their own ways, drawing on their own mathematical understandings and knowledge. As they work to solve these problems and to pose others for their classmates, they develop the very skills we've previously attempted to teach directly (though not necessarily in the order we might expect).

Deep understandings about number and operation develop as students work to make sense of challenging story problems, just as understandings about language grow as children read and write. The key to students' interest and engagement, however, appears to lie in the quality of the problems themselves. Problems that stretch children a bit beyond what they already know how to do or are open-ended enough to be solved in a variety of ways—*real* problems, in other words—invariably create more interest, involvement, and learning than drill and practice exercises masquerading as problems.

WHAT IS A *REAL* PROBLEM?

Simply stated, a *real* problem is a question for which there is no immediate answer (to the problem solver). In other words, a *real* problem is something your students don't already know how to do. In September, an addition problem such as:

> There are five children on the bus and four waiting at the next house. How many children will be on the bus after the next stop?

might pose a true problem-solving challenge to many first and second graders. Some will set five school kid counters on their bus boards, add four more and count the total starting from one. Others "count on" from five to arrive at nine. A few work from the fact that five plus five equals ten, reasoning that five plus four must be nine. For the handful who already know the answer, the story does not present a problem. The process of combining and separating sets becomes routine for most primary children rather quickly, however. While students may not know the answers immediately, stories involving addition and subtraction of numbers below ten cease to inspire much in the way of real problem solving; we must move on to more interesting situations if we wish to propel student learning. Stories that involve missing addends or subtrahends, comparison of quantities, multiplication, or division provide rich problem-solving challenges to most primary children throughout the fall months. Later in the year, some first graders and many second graders are ready to tackle problems that involve addition and subtraction of double digit numbers, partitioning, combined operations, or extraneous information.

The mark of a good problem is that it intrigues and inspires, accommodates a variety of strategies and tools, and sometimes involves more than one answer. Neal uses a picture and words to pose the following problem to his first grade classmates in April:

The store wants ten bears. How many do they need?
by Neal

While we adults might symbolize this problem as 3 + ? = 10 or 10 − ? = 3, Lisa solves it by means of a diagram, first showing three bears on the shelf and then continuing to draw bears until the total is ten.

For Lisa, making a sketch is an effective approach. Daniel, on the other hand, records a number sentence in response to the problem and notes that he is "thinking before you said." (See illustrations on following page.)

Is one method more advanced? Probably not; we've found that some children consistently solve problems by means of sketches and diagrams while

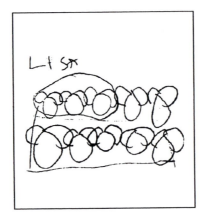

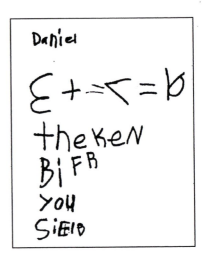

others work things out in their heads, tracking their progress with numbers or number sentences or figuring entire solutions mentally. Second graders demonstrate a similar range of strategies in response to a problem posed by one of their classmates in late spring:

> The Bear Store had 105 bears. Some people in Hawaii ordered 105 bears.
> The people in the bear store were going to deliver the bears in crates, but
> they didn't know how many crates. Can you help them? (Each crate holds 5
> bears.)

To us, this is a division problem. But these second graders don't know how to do division. That's why it's a *real* problem instead of a drill and practice exercise. Here's how they handle it:

Emily, who has used diagrams very effectively all year, counts upwards by fives until she reaches one hundred five, noting each five with a picture of a crate, and then counting the crates.

Breanna works in similar fashion, but uses numbers to track her progress, writing the multiples of five on her paper and then counting the numbers themselves.

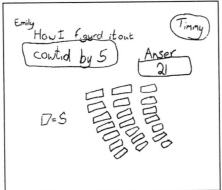

Emily

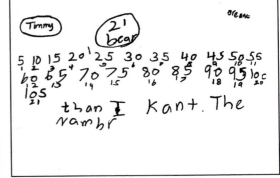

Breanna

Danny, who's more inclined to solve problems mentally, moves from a known fact (20 × 5 = 100) to the solution.

Timmy, who also enjoys working problems in his head whenever possible, applies a similar technique, noting that ten crates can hold fifty bears, so two sets of ten crates and one more, or twenty-one crates, will hold one hundred five bears.

<table>
<tr><td>

$\boxed{21}$

$\square = 5$

if you Taac 20 5's
=100 + 1 nor 5 = 21
craSe

</td><td>

21 becUS
hold "10 crats can
50 bears
16+10=20+1 more
50+50=100+5 = 21 / 105

</td></tr>
<tr><td style="text-align:center">**Danny**</td><td style="text-align:center">**Timmy**</td></tr>
</table>

Open-ended problems sometimes create an even greater challenge. The problem Danny poses to his second-grade classmates in April requires a good deal of thought, and ultimately proves impossible for some of the children.

> There were 2 crates of bears on the shelf in the store. Then a truck came with 10 more crates. Then there was a problem. Kids kept on coming in, so there were no more bears. So they got a truck to come in with 10 more crates. Then a boy came in with $50.00. All of the bears cost $4.00 and $3.00. How many can the boy buy altogether?

Although most of the students understand that the first five sentences are extraneous to the problem, they struggle to gain footholds. After reflecting

<table>
<tr><td>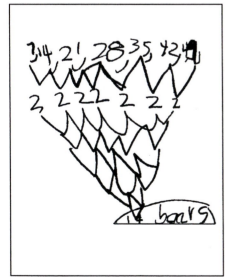</td><td>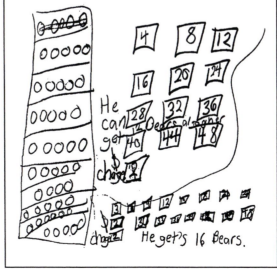</td></tr>
<tr><td style="text-align:center">**Ryan**</td><td style="text-align:center">**Faith**</td></tr>
</table>

that there are "all kinds of answers," Ryan decides to count upward by sevens—every time he purchases a three-dollar bear, he'll purchase a four-dollar bear too. In the end, he decides it's possible to buy fourteen bears with one dollar change.

Faith, on the other hand, decides to buy only four-dollar bears, and concludes that it's possible to purchase twelve bears with two dollars change. Then she experiments with buying only three-dollar bears, and finds she can purchase sixteen, with two dollars left over.

Breanna works and works, to no avail. First she counts by fives to fifty, but quickly realizes that this is not a helpful strategy. Next, she draws the store shelves loaded with fifty bears from the last shipment—she needs to see what the store looks like before she continues. Then she labels some of the bears with price tags, but it doesn't help.

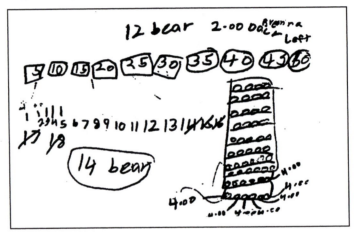

Breanna

Finally , she records some of the ideas she hears—twelve bears, fourteen bears—as children discuss their ideas and solutions. It's okay that she can't solve this problem; we've come to accept errors, misconceptions, and half-solutions as essential to the learning process. Because we are working with groups rather than individuals, all of the children have encountered problems they can't do or don't quite understand.

In any given session, we try to pose a range of problems varied enough to afford each student success as well as challenge. We often take a few minutes to discuss a problem, asking the children to explain to one another what it is they're trying to solve. We may share ideas of our own, but we try not to impose solutions or teach strategies. We've learned that our suggestions aren't always helpful to children. Still, we nestle in as needed to help them find a way to begin. Though we don't always succeed, we try to act as facilitators rather than answer-givers. The pay-off is in children's growing confidence and delight in their own mathematical·abilities.

HOW DOES PROBLEM SOLVING HELP CHILDREN
LEARN MATHEMATICS?

If you're still with us, you've probably realized that what we're proposing here is a fairly radical departure from traditional math instruction. In a nutshell, we are asking you to feed your students a steady diet of problems that are often a little too hard. Furthermore, we're asking you to avoid telling them how to handle these challenges. Children need time to develop their own mathematical strategies, although your encouragement and willingness to accept errors and misconceptions will be vital. You will also have to accept the fact that some of your students won't be able to solve every problem. If you are able to trust children's innate drive to grapple with things they don't quite understand, however, you will see a surprising amount of growth.

This is not as crazy as it sounds. Years ago, no one would have dreamed of asking first or second graders to write their own stories or research reports. How could children who didn't know how to spell or punctuate properly possibly write original compositions? We now understand that the best way to teach spelling, punctuation, and the many other skills that go into writing is by having our children write. And so we send them off, armed with pencils and crayons to write stories—in first grade! To begin with, some of them can only draw during Writers' Workshop and their stories don't appear to be stories at all, only disconnected pictures. Others use strings of random letters to accompany their drawings—they know that real stories have letters. A few have figured out that letters stand for certain sounds; they can spell phonetically if they listen to each word carefully enough and put down what they hear, but they often aren't able to leave spaces between their words.

We watch, we listen, we try to help a few, but mostly we stand back and encourage children to write their own stories in the best ways they know how. Within a few weeks, students are swapping theories about how to spell certain words, exchanging topic ideas, and sharing their stories with the group. By midyear, most children have made tremendous growth, even though their writing skills are still fairly rudimentary.

We believe the mathematical equivalent of asking primary children to write original compositions is to pose problems they don't already know how to solve. As in Writers' Workshop, some students will be more advanced than others; not every problem will be a *real* problem to every child, and a few will find many of the problems completely beyond their understanding.

That is why we revisit every type of problem in each theme. The same children who found missing addends impossible to understand in September may be writing such problems for their classmates in December. If only a third of your second graders are able to handle a partitioning problem with teddy bears, half of them may "get it" with cookies. If you pose challenging problems throughout the year and remain steadfast in your determination to encourage children's thinking, they will slowly begin to share strategies and theories as they explain their solutions, and may eventually astonish you with their mathematical creativity, growth in skills, and willingness to take risks.

ARE YOU CONCERNED ABOUT LETTING CHILDREN INVENT THEIR OWN WAYS TO SOLVE PROBLEMS?

This is an interesting question. If you ask a group of second graders to consider the problem of adding twenty-four and forty-eight cookies without teaching them how to add two-digit numbers first, they're almost sure to work with the tens before they deal with the ones. A typical approach to 24 + 48 might go something like this:

> Twenty plus forty is sixty. Then I've got the eight and the four. Well, sixty plus eight is sixty-eight, and four more is sixty-nine, seventy, seventy-one, seventy-two.

There are many variations on this theme, but most children will work from the front end of a problem, starting with the tens instead of the ones unless you instruct them to do otherwise. Such methods persist even into addition of three- and four-digit numbers:

> 358 + 487? Let's see...that's going to be somewhere around seven hundred, no eight hundred and something because I can see that three hundred plus four hundred will be seven hundred, and eighty-seven plus fifty-eight will be more than another hundred.

Students respond to subtraction of two-digit numbers in much the same way if they haven't had formal instruction in borrowing. A story problem that involves subtracting nineteen teddy bears from forty-five might draw the following response from a second-grader:

> 45 – 19...Hmmm...it's going to be around thirty, I think, because forty take away ten is thirty. But what about the five and the nine? You can't take nine away from five. Hmmm...

(At this point, the child might reach for dimes and pennies or base ten counting pieces.)

> Okay. Here's forty-five. Now, to take away nineteen, I can take a ten away. To get the nine, I'll just cover up nine squares on this ten stick. That leaves twenty-five...twenty-six. That's

funny—it's not thirty, but I wasn't too far off.

Another child might solve the problem by moving to numbers with which she is more familiar, and working from there:

> 45 – 19...that's almost like 45 – 20. 40 – 20 is 20, so 45 – 20 is 25, but the answer is really 26 because you're only taking away 19.

These methods are sometimes awkward and rather groping. Is there harm in letting children pursue them? We think not. We believe that allowing children to develop and discuss their own strategies, even if they don't match ours, actually enhances number sense and deepens students' understandings of such "big ideas" as place value, number relationships, and operations. Once standard algorithms are taught, it seems that many children cease to think about what they're doing. Adding sixty-seven and twenty-nine simply becomes a matter of applying someone else's formula; it ceases to present a *real* problem to many children, while becoming an unfathomable mystery to others.

So what about the standardized tests? Worse yet, what about third grade? What happens to our students then? Are they admired for their mathematical creativity and marvelous number sense, or punished for not knowing how to do things the "right way"? Since most standardized tests demand only the right answer but do afford children the luxury of scratch paper, our students usually don't suffer. As for third grade, we hope the practices advocated by Libby Pollett, Debby Head, and Michael Arcidiacono in *Opening Eyes to Mathematics* (MLC Publications, 1992) and Marilyn Burns in *All About Teaching Mathematics* (Math Solutions Publications, 1992), practices inspired by the NCTM Standards, become widespread in the very near future. Until then, you'll have to play it by ear. Teach standard methods if you feel you must, but try to put it off as long as possible. You may be amazed at some of the strategies your children invent when faced with *real* problems.

WHY USE STORY BOXES?

They help children see mathematics in relationship to their everyday lives.

In designing the story boxes, we chose themes that were both inherently mathematical and also common to young children's lives. Nearly every child has ridden in a bus of some sort and noted with interest the comings and goings of other riders.

The fantasy of Halloween is so powerful it inspires tremendous growth in children's oral and written language in our own classrooms every October. The appearance, disappearance, and capture of such imaginary creatures as ghosts and goblins, along with the whimsy of bright-eyed pumpkins in the window, never fail to spark children's imaginations. (We have included a second theme for October centered on night critters in the closet and under the bed, should Halloween be a theme you don't wish to address.)

We feel that most children have eagerly anticipated the arrival of presents for Christmas, birthdays, or other special occasions, counting how many they have and wondering how many more they're likely to receive. Finally, shopping for cookies and toys such as teddy bears seems to be a fairly universal experience, rich in mathematical possibilities.

Stories about these familiar situations allow young children access to mathematical operations they might not otherwise understand. While the number sentence $6 \div 2 = ?$ might draw blank stares from most first graders, there's not a child we know who hasn't experienced division first hand. The problem of sharing six cookies fairly with a friend brings almost instantaneous response from even the youngest school children. Usually one of each pair grabs all the cookies and doles them out ("One for you, one for me..."), but sometimes a child will make two piles of three ("You see—three and three is six—that's three for each of us!").

One point we want to make about these themes is that we've selected them not only because buying and sharing cookies or tracking the comings and goings of people, imaginary creatures, or presents help students understand mathematics, but also that *mathematics helps children understand how to share the cookies, buy the teddy bears, or keep track of the people on the bus.* In the words of the 1992 California State Mathematics Framework, "When mathematical ideas help students understand situations, the ideas are not only more interesting and accessible but also easier to remember and use."

Story problems are a natural forum for mathematical communication.

Although some authors write for themselves, stories are generally told to be heard or written to be read by others. Story problems also involve communication and the very best ones are posed with an actual audience in mind. Primary children enjoy solving story problems and sometimes explaining their strategies, but they take even more delight in posing problems for others. As with other forms of writing, their sense of audience is weak at first, but develops as the year progresses and they see classmates trying to solve *their* problems. Eventually, they draw or write with real purpose, attempting to entertain and challenge their friends.

Verbalizing or writing about one's strategies and solutions has become a highly valued practice in mathematics education, but can be difficult to pull off with young children. Admonitions to "Explain how you figured that out" or "Show me your thinking in words" sometimes fall on deaf ears. For one thing, it can be difficult to track and verbalize one's own thought processes. Sometimes children arrive at answers intuitively and explain themselves by saying, "I just knew it." Lack of writing skills can be another contributing factor; for some first and second graders, it's hard to write about anything at all. Another reason children sometimes resist explaining their ideas in writing is that some think more readily, or at least picture their thoughts more easily, in numbers or diagrams rather than words. (Albert Einstein once said that his ideas often came to him in pictures first, numbers next, and finally, maybe, in words.)

This is not to say that we don't ask children to explain their thinking. We stop frequently during problem-solving sessions to encourage children to share their thoughts and strategies with their classmates. We also ask students to find ways to express their thinking on paper, but we're careful to accept pictures and numbers as well as words. While we're fully aware of the insights individuals can gain when attempting to express their own thought processes, we've also discovered that young children may be more motivated to present their thoughts on paper for an audience of peers than for themselves or the teacher. Our second graders went to particular lengths to explain themselves clearly in a story problem exchange we did with another class. In the example below, Sara used numbers, words, and pictures to explain her thinking to JB, knowing that he would read and appreciate her comments.

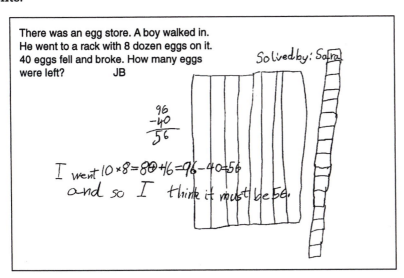

Story Boxes give children the support they need to be able to solve and pose a wide variety of story problems.

While older or more experienced students use visual models or manipulate abstract symbols to solve problems, young children often need to act things out. Full dramatization with students serving as the actors is a wonderful way to begin, but as problems move to higher quantities and greater complexity, small characters moved around on miniature backdrops become a more viable alternative. Lima bean school kids and tiny cardboard presents can be easily manipulated—hidden behind doors, placed on the mantel or under the tree, let on or off the bus, or divided evenly among several eager recipients. They can also be produced in sufficient quantity so each child can have his or her own to use for problem-solving sessions.

When students begin to pose their own problems, the counters and boards also lend support to the challenging task of developing mathematical stories. The Teddy Bear board shows shelves and a counter, along with a delivery truck, while the School Bus Kids board pictures a bus and a house with a door that opens and shuts. The Halloween board is a fence and a multi-storied house with many windows, while one of the Presents boards pictures a tree and a closet door. These are natural prompts for counting, comparing, adding, subtracting, multiplying, and dividing and allow children to pose problems in the form of pictures and symbols, long before they're able to actually write problems.

The Teddy Bear Store board   **School Bus Kids board**

   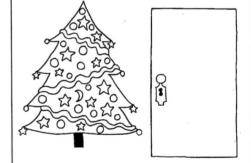

Trick or Treat board   **Christmas Presents board**

HOW ARE THE STORY BOX THEMES ORGANIZED?

First of all, it's important to understand that *Posing and Solving Problems with Story Boxes* is not meant to be an entire math program. To do a full job of helping our first and second graders develop pattern, spatial, number and operation sense, we also use the Calendar, the Concept Boxes, and many of the seasonal activities from *Box It or Bag It Mathematics*. The Story Box themes drive so much learning, though, that we spend five to seven days a month with them in September, October or November, and December, and five days or more per month in January, February, March, April, and May.

We begin with School Bus Kids in September. This theme, which revolves around children getting on and off the bus, enables us to pose addition, missing addend/subtrahend, multiplication, and division problems right away. Children solve the problems by acting them out and using School Bus Kid counters on storyboards. Those who are able explain their strategies. There is much imitating of peers' work as children who don't "get it" attempt to make sense of these challenges. (We take comfort in the fact that the only way some first graders can cope with Writers' Workshop in September and October is to copy anything they can find in print. Some of us have many student-authored versions of *Mrs. Wishy Washy* and *The Very Hungry Caterpillar* in our classrooms each fall!) We also introduce new terms such as "twice as many" and "half as many" knowing that at least a few students understand the concepts and will eventually help us teach the others.

After working orally for a session or two, we bring in written problems (problem models) to share with the students:

I've picked up four children so far. There should be half that number at this next stop. How many will be waiting? How many children will there be altogether?

❂ I have four on the bus. There should be twice that many at the next house. How many will be waiting? How many children will that make altogether?

Together, we look at the pictures first, trying to determine what problems are being posed. (It is especially important for our first graders to realize that they can pose problems in picture form.) Then we read the words that accompany our pictures and the children use their counters and boards to solve the problems. After sharing several different problem models, we ask our students to create their own School Bus Kids story problems. First graders usually work in picture form only, using a question mark to signal the problem to be solved. Second graders create their problems in picture form first and then write the words. In the beginning, we don't expect to see much more than copies of our problem models. Many children will modify the quantities and a few will come up with their own twists, but it may be two or three more units before things really start cooking. Once children have composed their own problems, they share them with their classmates, who work together to try to solve them. This instructional sequence, which we've summarized below, is repeated with every theme.

STORY BOX INSTRUCTIONAL SEQUENCE

Sessions 1 & 2   **Getting Started**
- Story problems are posed orally by the teacher.
- Students solve them using storyboards and counters, and share their ideas with one another.

Session 3   **Creating Story Problems: Examining Some Possibilities**
- Teacher presents story problems in written and picture form.
- Students examine the pictures and words to determine what problems are being posed, solve them using storyboards and counters, and share their ideas.

Session 4   **Creating Story Problems: Crafting Story Problems**
- Students create their own story problems, using our problem models for reference. Most first graders use pictures to pose their problems until spring. Second graders use pictures and words the entire year.

Sessions 5, 6 & 7   **Solving Student Problems**
- Student problems are shared with the class.
- Children are encouraged to use manipulatives, sketches, or "their heads" to solve problems. They record their strategies and solutions on paper, using pictures, numbers, and/or words.

Although the instructional sequence remains the same throughout the year, the problems don't. We recycle each type of problem with every theme, knowing that children's understandings will develop at different times, but we also introduce new types of problems and more challenging versions of earlier problems as the year progresses. We do gear the problems we pose to the abilities of our group and we've marked the most difficult ones with stars. You'll have to gauge your own students from year to year, but beware of underestimating your children.

We try to honor all levels of understanding in our own classrooms, but we figure if we're not losing at least a few students on some of the problems, we're probably working at a level that is too easy. The complexity and difficulty of the problems the children pose for one another change, moving from addition and subtraction of various sorts, through multiplication and division, and for second graders, to combined operations and problems containing extraneous information and/or very large numbers.

WHAT KINDS OF MATERIALS WILL I NEED TO IMPLEMENT THESE ACTIVITIES?

You will need to make five story boxes and five sets of problem models to teach these lessons. Each story box includes a class set of storyboards and about four hundred teacher-produced counters. The storyboards and problem models can be copied directly from the blacklines in this book and require very little time to prepare. The sets of counters are another matter, but once they're made, they'll last for several years. (Or purchase colored, punchout carboard counters from The Math Learning Center, see page 182.) If you have an overhead projector and enjoy using it to present whole-group lessons to your class, you'll also want to make an overhead transparency of each storyboard and a small set of overhead counters for each theme.

In addition to the story boxes and problem models, you'll need Unifix cubes and/or 1" square colored plastic tile. We also recommend that children, especially second graders, have access to base ten counting pieces and calculators (we've found that a half-class set of calculators is adequate).

Finally, students will need writing paper, construction paper, glue, scissors, scotch tape, and other common school supplies to create and solve story problems. You will find complete instructions for making story boxes and problem models, preparing needed print materials and overhead transparencies, and ordering auxilliary manipulatives at the end of this book under Preparation of Materials.

WHAT IF THE FIRST GRADE TEACHERS IN MY BUILDING HAVE ALREADY USED THIS BOOK?

Even if your students have used story boxes in kindergarten and gone through all the themes in first grade, you can still use *Posing and Solving Problems with Story Boxes.* Although some of the problems in the first three themes will be easy for some students, they will discover new strategies and continue to develop good number sense. The same children who solved addition problems by counting on in first grade may now arrive at a solution to "nine children on the bus, four more got on" by thinking of the four as three and the nine as ten. Youngsters who solved missing addend problems by counting cookies or teddy bears may think in terms of subtraction this time around.

Gauge your group carefully in September. If the School Bus addition and subtraction problems seem too easy for most of your second graders, substitute larger numbers or move into multiplication and division sooner. Many second graders love the patterning problems in October and will be able to go much further with them than they did in first grade; but if the Halloween computation problems don't seem to pack enough punch, have a look at some of the money and partitioning problems in the last two units and adapt them to fit the theme. Remember, also, the problems marked with a star are for you—it's unlikely that your children will have done them in first grade.

Finally, be assured that your students will be eager to pose challenges for their classmates when they write their own problems. We've seen many first graders and some second graders persist in writing simple addition and subtraction stories long after we've posed and modeled more complex operations because their comfort level simply hasn't yet progressed beyond that. When their classmates solve these problems with ease, however, they vow to make it a little harder next time. No matter how much experience your students have had with story boxes, you will need to continue to pose problems at many different levels throughout the year.

WHAT KINDS OF ASSESSMENT OPPORTUNITIES DO STORY BOXES PROVIDE?

"Mathematics assessment in the 1990s will focus increasingly on assessing large pieces of work rather than smaller ones. Assessment and instruction will be integrated more effectively. Teachers can raise standards and expectations, asking thoughtful questions that allow for thoughtful (and unexpected) responses....Most important, teachers can learn to...focus on what students know rather than on what they don't know."

"Assessment provides teachers with a window into students' thinking and understanding, as well as into their proficiency with more narrow skills, and reveals the quality of the students' mathematical communication. It also helps teachers evaluate the success of the mathematics program and provides information helpful in making decisions on instruction."

Mathematics Framework for California Public Schools

If you regard math assessment as a process of making discoveries about children's preferred tools and strategies for solving problems, as well their understandings of pattern, number, and operation, you'll find the activities in this book provide some wonderful opportunities to learn more about your students and for your students to learn more about themselves. Children's explanations of how they solve various problems throughout the year are particularly revealing. While youngsters' verbal explanations of their problem-solving strategies during class discussions can be difficult to capture, we find that we begin to develop intuitive understandings about our students during the first few months of school by simply listening to them.

In September, the problem

> There are eight children on the bus. The driver will pick up three more at the next stop. How many will be on the bus then?

elicits a variety of responses from first graders. Many children set eight School Bus Kid counters on their bus, put three more behind the door, and count the total starting from one. Others do the same but count on from three or eight. Still others arrive at a total by counting from one, three, or eight on their fingers. A few seem to know the total instantly and might even verbalize something as sophisticated as the fact that eight plus two is ten, so one more will be eleven. A few may get snarled up in the process of counting eight accurately or combining the sets of eight and three, and may not be able to arrive at a total at all.

Second graders may respond in equally diverse ways. A missing addend problem such as

> There are six kids on the bus. The bus driver thought that he would have fourteen kids on the bus after this stop. How many got on?

might prompt some children to set out six counters on the bus portions of their storyboards and continue slipping beans under the door flaps of their houses until they reach a total of fourteen. They open the doors then and count the beans they've slipped under the flaps, to discover that it takes eight more to make fourteen.

Others accomplish the same task on their fingers, starting from six and counting on until they reach fourteen by holding up eight. Still others raise their hands immediately, explaining they know the answer because six kids plus eight kids are fourteen, or fourteen take away six is eight, or seven kids and seven kids are fourteen, and since there are six on the bus, there must be eight waiting behind the door to get on.

This might not be enough information about our students to be very helpful initially, but as we pose problems throughout the fall, patterns begin to emerge. It becomes clear that some children solve most problems by setting them up on their storyboards with counters. Others will make use of their fingers. Still others appear to work mentally. Some of them are able to explain their thinking quite clearly, while others can only tell you they "just knew it." Some children seem quite comfortable with a variety of methods, while others seem more heavily invested in one particular method. Some students seem to solve every problem by counting one by one, while others appear to think in fives or tens or to work from facts they already know.

Eventually, we begin to get a sense of the tools children choose in problem solving as well as their preferred strategies. We also attempt to share our perceptions with the students themselves during problem-solving sessions, reflecting back what we notice without judging one method to be better than another. We think it's important for children to be aware of the many different ways problems can be solved, but also to be aware of their own current inclinations. Clara knows that right now fingers are an effective and very acceptable tool for her, even though Johnny and Sara prefer to use boards and counters and Rachel usually solves problems in her head.

In addition to asking children to share their solutions and strategies orally, we have them present their strategies on paper. This makes it even easier to get a handle on student thinking. Although their pictures, words, and numbers don't necessarily tell the whole story, they do offer some insights we can hang on to. We can collect their papers, reflect back on the problems, and try to remember who used the beans and boards and who reached for the tile or base ten counting pieces instead.

It becomes evident that some children use diagrams or sketches of one sort or another to solve problems, while others work almost exclusively in their heads, recording their thinking in numbers or words. Sometimes we like to lay out all the responses to a particular problem side by side, looking again for trends and patterns. Neal, a first grader, poses a story problem for his classmates by showing three bears on a shelf and a truck approaching the store. He writes, "The store wants ten bears. How many more do they need?"

Rutta responds by drawing three bears and then continuing until she has a

Rutta

total of ten. She then goes back and counts the additional bears to determine that seven more are needed to produce a total of ten. The diagram she's drawn is instrumental in helping her solve the problem.

Steven responds by drawing three bears on the shelves. Then he labels them "1, 2, 3" and continues writing four through ten on the truck to indicate the truck will be delivering seven more. (Illustrations are on the next page for this comment and the next three comments.)

Lucian uses the same strategy but adds a number sentence to reinforce his conclusion.

Melissa holds the three in her head and draws enough bears to make a total of ten. It's possible that she figured it out mentally first, wrote the number 7, drew seven bears to illustrate her point, and finished off with a number sentence, but we couldn't be sure of her sequence unless we asked.

Like Melissa, Cory holds the three in his head, but indicates in his response that he counted on his fingers to reach ten.

Steven

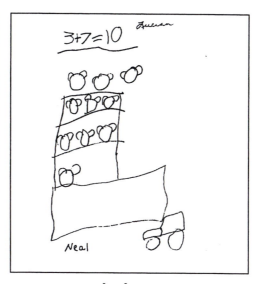

Lucian

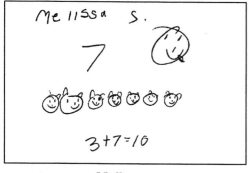

Melissa

Cory

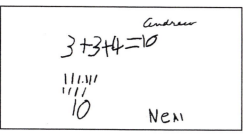

Andrew

Andrew works by means of tally marks, recording a rather elaborate number sentence for ten when he's finished.

While it's fascinating to observe the diversity of responses in a group, we might also make observations about individuals, especially if we examine work produced over several months. The collection of work shown on the next page reinforces our notion that Danny, a second grader, is a child who likes to work things out in his head. He thinks in chunks of five, ten, or one hundred whenever possible, often using his fingers to keep track of what he's doing. He presents his thinking in numbers and words, but notice that he uses words to take the place of mathematical symbols he doesn't yet know.

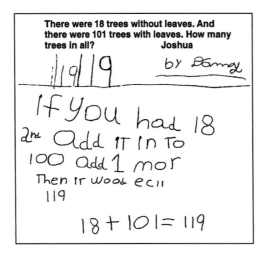

There were 18 trees without leaves. And there were 101 trees with leaves. How many trees in all?   Joshua

by Danny

119

If you had 18
2nd Add it in To
100 add 1 mor
Then it wood ecll
119

18 + 101 = 119

A man bought a dozen and a half chocolate chip cookies. How much did it cost?

90¢

I wpnt BY
fives on
my fegrs

The work lady made 31 cookies and she had a telephone call, and when she was on the telephone another lady went in and put some of the cookies in the oven. When she came back, she only saw 7 on the counter. How many more are in the oven?
by Breanna
Danny

24

31 − 7 = 24

How I dp pt
at frst I had
31 and − 5 and − 2 mor
and pt ecld 24

The Bear Store had 105 bears. Some people in Hawaii ordered 105 bears. The people in the bear store were going to deliver the bears in crates, but they didn't know how many crates. Can you help them?
(Each crate holds 5 bears.)

□ = 5   21

if you Tooc 20 5's
= 100 + 1 mor 5 = 21
clase

Danny

A small boy bought three chocolate chip cookies and five sugar cookies. How much did he have to pay?

he Pay 35

5 + 5 + 5 = 15 + 4 + 4 + 4 + 4 = 35

By analyzing the collection of work above, we can see that Danny's preferred tools for solving problems are his head and his fingers—he does not usually use other manipulatives or sketches at all. We can also see that he consistently chooses to present his thinking in numbers and words. Furthermore, we can make some observations about his strategies and math skills. Danny appears to rely heavily on counting and thinking in chunks of five, ten, and one hundred. He counts easily by fours, fives, and tens and counts on when he's not sure what comes next. He seems to have a good command of addition and subtraction, and uses these operations to solve multiplication and division problems. Although we cannot base our entire picture of Danny's mathematical thinking on this collection of work, we're able to learn quite a bit about him by watching what he does with story problems.

While Danny seems determined to solve problems mentally, Faith, another second grader, uses manipulatives of various sorts, diagrams, and mental arithmetic with equal comfort. She seems to choose her tools in response to the type or perhaps the perceived difficulty of each problem. In her first work sample, Faith sets out thirteen tiles to represent the thirteen books. Then she adds eight plus eight plus eight. She concludes that the man can buy three books for twenty-five dollars with one dollar left over. She presents her thinking in pictures, numbers, and words.

In response to Danny's problem about the boy who walks into the teddy bear store with fifty dollars to spend on three- and four-dollar bears *(How many can he buy?)*, Faith first draws a picture of the store shelves. When her first sketch doesn't help, she counts by fours, using a diagram to help track her progress. Once she's up to forty-eight dollars, she goes back and counts the number of fours to determine that the boy can buy twelve bears with two dollars left over. She repeats the process with threes next.

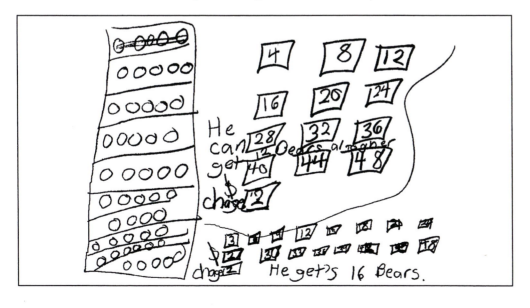

21

Faith uses pennies and nickels to solve both of the problems below. For the first, she sets out twelve nickels and then six more, and counts by fives to arrive at her answer. In the second, she sets out fifty pennies, pulls away seven groups of four to represent the amount the man had to pay, and counts the remainder to determine how much change he should receive.

A man bought a dozen and a half choco-late chip cookies for 5¢ each. How much did it cost altogether?	Sugar cookies cost 4¢ each. The man wanted seven of them. He gave the clerk two quarters. How much change should he get?

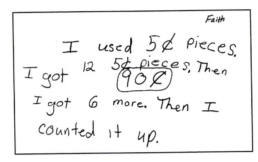

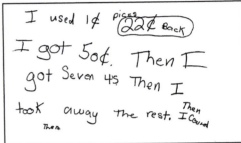

To solve Mark's cookie problem below, Faith writes that she "counted 19 + 35". It's unclear how she actually arrived at the total of fifty-four (did she count on from thirty-five?) until you look carefully at her paper and note the erasures which read "10 + 30 = 40 + 5 = 45." These notes make it clear that Faith added nineteen and thirty-five by working with the tens first, adding on the five, and probably counting nine up from forty-five to arrive at fifty-four. Sometimes children's erasures or cross-outs are more informative than their finished products!

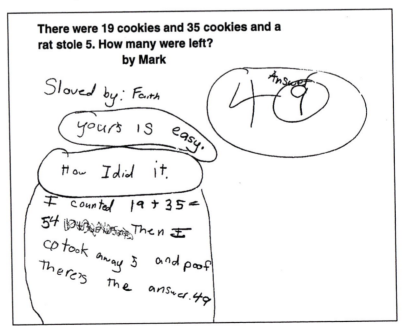

Again, we can use Faith's work samples to make some generalizations about her mathematical thinking. First of all, she'll use any tool she needs to get the job done, including sketches, manipulatives, and mental arithmetic. Like Danny, she relies heavily on counting strategies, and seems to be able to count by fives and tens easily. She understands place value well enough to come up with an efficient way to solve 19 + 35. The fact that she converts two quarters to fifty pennies to make change causes us think she might not be as adept at thinking in chunks when it comes to subtraction or, perhaps, the quarters themselves have created some discomfort for her.

Faith seems to have a solid grip on the processes of addition and subtraction and handles multiplication as a process of repeated addition. She presents her work in pictures, numbers, and words, but her ability to talk her way through problems is rather striking. This is a very significant discovery for us, but it's even more important for Faith. The awareness that she can use her strength in language to help her with mathematics could have tremendous significance throughout her school years.

While Danny seems to specialize in numbers and Faith uses language, some of our children employ sketches and diagrams to solve problems. This is an interesting and powerful brand of thinking. As Emily, another second-grader, responds to Sara's problem about the mom who buys twenty-five bears for her eight children *[how many do they each get?]*, we see her instantly draw eight circles, one to represent each child. She then distributes tally marks among all the circles until she reaches twenty-four and concludes that each child can have three bears with one left over.

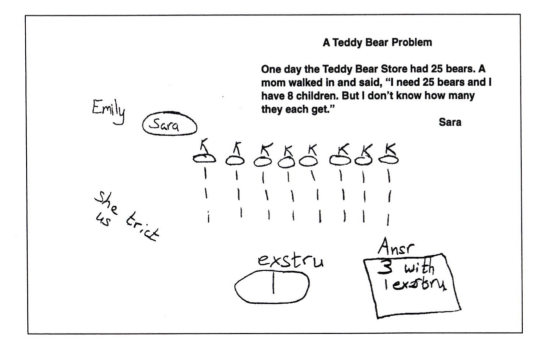

A Teddy Bear Problem

One day the Teddy Bear Store had 25 bears. A mom walked in and said, "I need 25 bears and I have 8 children. But I don't know how many they each get."

Sara

Emily

Sara

She us trict

exstru

Ansr
3 with
1 exsbru

23

Some students do the same thing with manipulatives, but Emily's work is distinguished in that she turns immediately to pictures to solve challenging problems. Our impression of her as a sort of "spatial" or visual problem solver is reinforced by observations of her work in areas such as art and science too.

While we can't give you a precise recipe for assessment, we can tell you that we've learned a great deal about our children by listening and watching carefully as they solve problems throughout the year and by saving and analyzing their written explanations. We find that from students' work with Story Boxes, we can pull information about preferred problem-solving tools, preferred methods of presentation, strategies, and some specific math skills. When we combine this information with observations we make of students' responses during Calendar, whole-group lessons, and independent work sessions, we wind up with fairly comprehensive portraits of children's mathematical thinking. These understandings can then be used to plan and modify future instruction, to explain children's strengths and needs to parents and other concerned adults, and to promote self-knowledge among students. As you listen to children's explanations and examine their written responses to real problems throughout the year, we know you'll discover many exciting things about your own students.

School Bus Kids

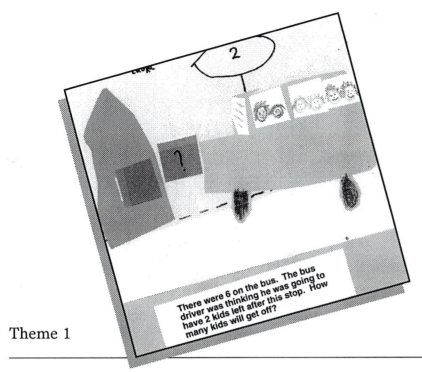

There were 6 on the bus. The bus driver was thinking he was going to have 2 kids left after this stop. How many kids will get off?

School Bus Kids

T his theme draws on the familiar experience of riding a school bus to introduce the idea of solving and posing story problems in September. Because a bus fills on its way to school and empties on the way back, the possibilities for posing problems involving addition, subtraction, multiplication, and division are almost endless:

> The big yellow bus pulls up and six children get on. If they sit in pairs, how many seats will they fill? Down the road they go. The bus stops at the corner of 24th and Main and four more children get on. How many children are on the bus now and how many seats have they filled? The bus driver is quite familiar with her route and knows there will be fifteen children on the bus after she stops at the Courtside Apartments. How many will be getting on at that stop?

We have found that even children who don't ride a bus to school take much interest and delight in tracking the comings and goings of passengers, first on an imaginary bus we set up in the classroom with two rows of chairs and then using tiny lima bean "kid" characters on small school bus storyboards. Once children have had ample opportunity to enact our story problems, we help them develop their own to share with classmates. The entire process takes about seven school days and is just the first step in a year-long series of encounters with story problems.

Getting Started

TELLING STORIES / DRAMATIC PLAY

You will need...

- 12 classroom chairs set up in pairs, plus a driver's seat
- a baseball cap, a pair of sunglasses, a large name tag, or some other way of identifying the bus driver
- a feely box of students' names. p. 192
- Unifix cubes, 12 per student

We suggest you introduce this theme by eliciting experiences from your students about riding buses. In this discussion, you might address some of the following questions: What are the safety rules on a school bus? How are children expected to board a bus? Why do drivers often ask children to load from back to front and unload from front to back? Afterward, have students set up thirteen classroom chairs in two columns of six with a driver's seat at the front to play-act an imaginary bus ride as you narrate the story below. Children in the audience may solve the problems you pose along the way using any number of strategies, but some will appreciate access to Unifix cubes.

> It was early in the morning when the bus driver (pull a name from the feely box) completed her safety check and started the engine (children add sound effects). She carefully pulled away from the bus yard and began thinking how happy she'd be to see the children again today. At the first stop, three children (pull three more cards from the feely box) climbed onto the bus. As she drove along, she knew there would be two children (feely box) waiting at the next stop.

How many students will be on the bus once they get on?

> The next corner was the stop at the Sunny Oaks Apartments. Her load was about to double.

How many children do you think will be getting on? How could you figure it out? (Use the feely box to identify five more passengers once children have solved the problem.)

> The bus was nearly full with all those bouncing children, but there was still the stop at the mobile home park where two more youngsters (feely box) would be picked up. The bus driver was trying to remember how many were already on the bus.

Can you help her? And when two more get on, how many children will there be in all?

> As they reached the school, the driver asked the children in the front two rows of seats to get off first.

How many will be getting off? How many children will still be on the bus?

> The next two rows were asked to get off.

Who should stand?

> And finally, the remaining children climbed off as the driver called out, "Have a good day. See you after school."

Most of your students will want to continue this activity until they've all had at least one turn to "ride the bus". You might tell a variation of the story immediately or come back to the theme later in the day. Students can be encouraged to take turns narrating some of the bus stories too, especially if you use related literature to help prime the language of comings and goings. We've listed a few of our favorites below:

Mr. Gumpy's Outing by John Burningham (1971)

Ten in a Bed by Mary Rees (1988)

How Many Are in This Old Car? by Colin and Jacqui Hawkins (1988)

What Do You Do With a Kangaroo? by Mercer Mayer (1987)

Rooster's Off to See the World by Eric Carle (1987)

BASIC OPERATIONS WITH STORYBOARDS & COUNTERS

You will need...

- an overhead of each School Bus Kids storyboard, p.190; Blacklines B5-B6

- 13 overhead School Bus Kids, p.190; Blackline B1

- School Bus Kids storyboards, 1 copy of each per child, p.188; Blacklines B5-B6

- School Bus Kid counters, 13 per child, p.184

Now that the theme has been set and children are thinking in terms of arrivals and departures, pose the problems below. Ask students to work with their storyboards and lima bean characters to set up and solve the problems, but don't insist on the use of these manipulatives by all students if some are able to work mentally at times. (This is more likely to occur among second graders than first.) As your students solve the problems, encourage them to share their different strategies at the overhead.

It will probably take two class sessions, possibly longer, to cover this set of problems. Second grade teachers may want to skip a few of the very easiest examples and emphasize the starred problems, while first grade teachers may find the non-starred examples provide adequate challenge. Don't worry if you "lose" some of your students along the way; we find that a few of ours tend to fade in and out but always return as long as the level of problem solving is broad enough to keep things interesting.

How Many Altogether?

● The driver has already picked up five children. He knows two more are waiting at the next house. How many children will be on the bus altogether?

✪ There are seven children sitting in the back of the bus and five more waiting to get on. How many will be on the bus altogether?

Adding Three or More Numbers

✪ The bus driver picked up three children at the first stop and five at the second. Three more were waiting at the last house on the block. How many children were on the bus altogether?

How Many Are Left?

● There were six children on the bus after a busy day at school. The driver stopped at the house and three got off. How many were left on the bus?

✪ Eleven children were peering out the windows of the bus, eager to get home to play. Seven got off at the first stop. How many were still on the bus?

Missing Addends / Missing Subtrahends

● It was a good day at school but the children were tired and eager to get home to their families. Before that last stop, the driver had eight children on the bus. Now there were only three. How many had gotten off?

✪ The bus was bustling with cheerful children, eight altogether. But the driver knew there had been thirteen on the bus before her last stop. How many children had gone into that last house?

Comparing or Finding The Difference

● The driver had picked up four children for the trip to the zoo. Three more were waiting to board. How many more children were on the bus than waiting to get on?

Twice As Many

● There are two children on the bus and twice as many waiting at the next house. How many children are waiting? How many will there be in all?

✪ There are four bouncing kids already on the bus. Twice as many are waiting at the next house. How many are waiting? How many will be on the bus in all?

Half As Many

● There are six cute kindergarten kids riding home from their first day of school. Half of them will get off at the next stop to go to their baby sitter. How many will be getting off at the next stop?

✪ Finally it was time for the big field trip. Eight children were waiting to get on the bus. Half that many had already been seated. How many were already on the bus? How many would there be altogether?

Division: Sharing / Grouping

● A mom was waiting for the bus to return from the night program. It was so dark when the bus pulled up that all she could see were eight tired eyes gazing down at her. How many children were on the bus?

✪ Twelve children got on the bus for the field trip to the potato chip factory. The driver asked them to sit three to a seat. How many seats did they need?

Creating Story Problems

In September, we present models of story problems in both pictures and words (*problem models*), which children examine and then solve. After working with our examples, children go on to create their own story problems. Most copy or modify our ideas only a little, while a few are able to invent their own pictorial, written, or mathematical twists. Although nearly all second graders can be expected to write stories to accompany their first picture problems, most first graders will be far more comfortable posing story problems in picture form only.

EXAMINING SOME POSSIBILITIES

You will need...

• School Bus Kids problem models, pp. 188-189; Blacklines B7-B18

• School Bus Kids storyboards, 1 copy of each per student, pp. 187-188; Blacklines B5-B6

• School Bus Kids counters, 13 per student, p. 184

If you are a second grade teacher, consider omitting the first two problem models and featuring the three marked with a star. You'll notice that our problem models aren't quite as challenging as some of the examples in the Getting Started section. This is because they're meant to help children write their own story problems. We find that most primary student aren't able to pose problems at quite the level they can solve them. If you are a first grade teacher, you'll probably want to limit your choice of problem models to the first four; more than that may prove overwhelming when children try to

choose models on which to base their own problems.

Begin by asking children to examine the picture portion of one of your problem models. Can they figure out what the problem is by looking at the picture alone? Show them the written story problem on the flap. Does the story help to clarify the problem to be solved?

First Grade Teacher: I have some new bus problems for you to solve today, but these are in picture form. As you look at this picture, what do you think it's asking you to figure out?

Children: It says five on the door. You can see five kids on the bus. There are some looking out the windows of that house. One, two, three, four, five. The driver can see them too. They're waiting for the bus. The driver's trying to figure out how many kids are going to be on the bus. Five and five. One, two, three, four, five, six, seven, eight, nine, ten. There will be ten!

Teacher: Let's peek at the story flap part. I'll read it to you:

There are five children on the bus and five waiting at the next house. How many children will be on the bus?

Children: That's just like the picture. It's ten. We already knew it. We just looked at the picture.

Teacher: You did that very well. Would people be willing to share how they arrived at their solutions.

Lisa: I counted on my fingers. See, I started with one and got to five on this hand—that's like the kids already on the bus. Then I counted to five on this hand. That's like the kids looking out the windows.

Teacher: How did you know how many would be on the bus altogether when the bus picked up those five children?

Lisa: I just knew.

It may be difficult for some of your students to explain their thinking to others. Nevertheless, we start asking right away, knowing that it's discussion and interaction among students that eventually propels much of their learning. As math educator Ernst von Glasersfeld puts it so beautifully,

> "...the teacher's attempts to understand the individual student's approach to a problem generate a climate of positive social interaction. Genuine interest in how they think shows the students, better than any verbal affirmation, that they are being taken seriously; and this, in turn, enhances their courage to try and openly discuss new paths of whose outcome they are still uncertain. There is no more efficient way to generate the kind of reflection that is necessary for conceptual advancement."

First Grade Teacher: Sometimes it's difficult to explain how you figured something out. Did anyone have a different way?

Melissa: I saw five in the window of the bus. Then I just used my fingers and I kept on counting.

Teacher: So did you say, "five, six, seven, eight, nine, ten"?

Melissa: No, I just thought about five on this hand, then I said, "six, seven, eight, nine, ten."

Alexis: I just know that five and five make ten. My dad taught me!

Michael: I used the bean kids. I put five in the bus and then I just moved those other five from the house onto the bus with them. Then I counted them. See—one, two, three, four, five, six, seven, eight, nine, ten.

Have students examine each of your problem models, discussing, reading, and solving the problems as they go. We find that some children are able to solve our picture/word problems mentally in the process of examining them, but they can certainly use the lima bean School Bus Kids counters and storyboards if they need them. Once all your problem models have been examined, display them in a prominent area at eye level so students can think

31

about which they might like to copy or modify when they create their own story problems.

SCHOOL BUS KIDS PROBLEM MODELS

To make copies of these problem models for use in your own classroom, see Preparation of Materials and Blacklines B7-B18.

Problem Model 1

If there are three children behind that door and three children already on the bus, how many children will I have altogether?

Problem Model 2

There are five children on the bus and five waiting at the next house. How many children will be on the bus after the next stop?

32

SCHOOL BUS KIDS PROBLEM MODELS (CONT.)

Problem Model 3

I know I had eight on the bus before that last stop. Now there are only six. How many got off?

Problem Model 4

I've picked up four children so far. There should be half that number at this next stop. How many will be waiting? How many children will there be altogether?

SCHOOL BUS KIDS PROBLEM MODELS (CONT.)

✪
**Problem
Model 5**

✪ I have four on the bus. There should be twice that many at the next house. How many will be waiting? How many children will that make altogether?

✪
**Problem
Model 6**

✪ What a wonderful field trip! It's too dark though. I can only see their eyes. I've got to figure out how many children are on this bus. Can someone help me?

SCHOOL BUS KIDS PROBLEM MODELS (CONT.)

○
**Problem
Model 7**

○ **What beautiful, bright-eyed children! So far, nine children are on the bus. How many bright eyes does that make? Four more children are waiting at the next house. When I pick them up, how many bright eyes will there be altogether?**

Crafting Story Problems

You will need...

- 9" x 12" light blue construction paper, 1 sheet per student, *or* School Bus Kids storyboard blacklines, 1 copy per student (see Note below)
- precut lima bean shapes in a variety of skin tones, 10+ per student, p. 191
- white construction paper in various small sizes to make "talking bubbles" for question marks, words, and numbers that signal problems to be solved
- 2" x 2³⁄₄" brown construction paper door flaps, 1 per student
- precut rectangles, squares, and triangles for houses, windows, etc., in a variety of colors*
- 6" x 8" yellow construction paper for buses, 1 per student*
- 2" x 8" black construction paper for wheels & bus windows, 2 per student*
- 3" x 9" green construction paper for landscape*
- 1¹⁄₂" x 4" pieces of brown for tree trunks, etc.*
- ultra-fine Sharpie pens, glue, scissors, crayons, and marking pens to share
  additional materials for second graders:
- 4¹⁄₂" x 12" light blue construction paper for story flaps, if your students are working from scratch, 1 per student*
- student writing paper and pencils

35

*Note: Before you gather the materials to have your children create their own story problems, think about whether you want them to start from scratch using light blue construction paper backgrounds or whether you want them to start with copies of the School Bus Kids storyboards. Starting with copies of the storyboards is somewhat easier, in that children only have to color in the buses and houses and add bean characters, but we truly enjoy the delightful buses, houses, and extra landscape touches that children like Jacob, whose work is shown below, create on their own. If you decide to have students create their story problems from scratch, you'll need the items marked with asterisks (*) above, **in addition to** the other materials listed.*

The bus driver is thinking he is going to have 8, and there are 4. How many are behind the door?

When all the problem models have been examined and solved, display them where children can easily refer to each kind as they create their own problems for others to solve. This early in the school year, you'll find that most students will copy your models almost exactly, changing only the numbers. Given that the task of presenting a story problem in written and/or pictorial form is probably a new and unfamiliar task to most, this is to be expected. Or, if your second graders worked with these materials last year, you'll probably see some marvelous twists, especially if you encourage them to create problems that will interest and challenge their classmates.

Explain that you want each child to prepare a School Bus Kids picture problem to pose to the rest of the class. It is important that the picture portion pose the problem as clearly as possible. Second graders will write a story problem to accompany their picture. (Most second graders will need some instruction from you and an additional day to work on the written portions of their problems.) You might set some limits on the number of bean characters children can use in their story problems. We held our first graders to ten or less and our second graders to fifteen.

Second Grade Teacher: Let's take a look at Sara's picture. What do you think she wants you to figure out?

Children: There are six kids on the bus. Three in each window. But the guy is thinking fourteen. There aren't fourteen kids on the bus!

Ryan: Wait! There's a question mark on the door, and you can tell that it opens. She must want us to figure out how many kids are going to get on.

Sara: That's it. You have to figure out how many kids are behind the door.

Brenton: That's easy—it's eight!

Teacher: Sara's picture is really very clear, but how could she put her problem into words?

Children: She could say that the bus driver was going to pick up some more kids. He knows he'll have fourteen when the kids behind that door get on. She could say there are six already on the bus.

Teacher: Those are all good ideas. What question will Sara have to pose at the end of her problem; what is it she wants people to figure out?

Children: How many are behind the door? How many got on? How many are going to come out of the house?

Teacher: Great! Once Sara finishes writing her problem, I want her to read it to a friend and ask her friend if it makes sense. When she's made any needed corrections, she'll bring it to me so I can get it typed tonight. Tomorrow, she'll glue it to a story flap so everyone will be able to read it.

When children's story problems are complete, encourage them to check with classmates to see if their work makes sense. Can other children understand what needs to be solved? Have they posed problems that can be solved by peers? Finally, have youngsters meet with you for final conferencing or editing as needed. Some first graders may need to explain their thinking to you and may even want to dictate a written portion. Second graders may need to refine a question or clarify their story in some way.

That evening, if possible, second grade teachers will need to type or print each child's problem on a 3½" x 11" strip of white paper, using standard spelling and punctuation. Since we both have Macintosh computers, we like to use a bold 36 point font with a sideways page setup. That way, we can type the whole batch of story problems at once, print them out, and cut them apart. Most computers have at least a 24 point font, if not a 36, but if you don't have access to a computer, you can print children's problems with a black felt tip marker. The point is to wind up with good quality print large enough to be read at a distance.

The next day, have children glue the typed or printed strips to their story flaps (see "You will need" list). Then tape the flaps to their pictures along the bottom on the backside. If your second graders used blacklines of the School Bus Kids storyboard to create their problems, they can just tape the typed strips directly to the bottoms of their pictures.

Also, have each child glue the draft copy of his or her writing to the back of his or her picture. Incorporating the rough draft into a finished product validates children's hard work and can be a nice source of information about students' growing capabilities in the areas of writing and spelling.

The bus driver is thinking he is going to have 8, and there are 4. How many are behind the door?

Jacob

The BuS GIVer es TeKeN heIS Go To hAV 8 he r WAPhAS4 h ow MaNY ISBe hIP The Do o r ?

Solving Student Problems

You will need...

- student story problems (We display each piece quickly and then have children work 3 or 4 of the more interesting or challenging examples.)
- half sheets of ditto paper and pencils, along with hard writing surfaces (clipboards or student chalkboards are fine)
- School Bus Kids storyboards and counters
- overheads of the School Bus Kids storyboards, along with overhead counters if you want children to demonstrate their strategies to one another

Once children have completed their own story problems, it's sharing time. Many first and second graders will be so anxious to see their own work displayed that they will hardly be able to focus on the problems you've selected for them to work. We recommend, therefore, that you allow youngsters to view each and every student piece before you begin.

After everyone's work has been admired by the group, seat children on the rug with writing materials and easy access to storyboards and bean characters. As students work through each problem you present, ask them to explain the various ways they are finding solutions and then encourage them to record their thinking via illustrations, numbers, and/or words. Expect some conversation among children and plenty of looking around and imitation on the part of those who don't yet "get it".

Many students will be delighted to use the beans and storyboards or their fingers as they solve problems, while others may use sketches or number sentences. Written solutions will be somewhat rudimentary this early in the year, but if youngsters are able to record their thinking in any form, be sure to tuck it into portfolios for future assessment purposes. You'll want to be an especially astute observer of your first graders this time around. If it seems too difficult for them to record their thoughts on paper, concentrate on oral and perhaps overhead explanations instead.

First Grade Teacher: What do you notice about Kittrina's problem?

Children: It's good! I like that bus. The bus driver has glasses. The driver has a seven over his head. It's like in Garfield and Snoopy when they're talking or thinking about something. See how it goes from the driver's head? Over on the house door it has that mark. Maybe he's trying to figure out how many kids used to be on his bus. Or maybe he wants to know how many there will be when more get on.

Teacher: What do you want them to figure out, Kittrina?

Kittrina: The driver is listening to the radio. Some kids got off.

Teacher: How many kids used to be on the bus?

Kittrina: Seven.

Michael: But now there are only three on the bus—see? One, two, three.

Kristen: She wants us to figure out how many are behind the door!

Teacher: Is that right, Kittrina?

Kittrina: Yes!

Jessica: Four!

Teacher: How did you figure that out?

Jessica: I just counted one, two, three, four, five, six, seven.

Teacher: But how do you know there are four children behind the door?

Jessica: Well, there are three over here, and then you go four, five, six, seven.

Matthew: I just looked at the three and went four, five, six, seven.

Jessie: I just know that three and four make seven.

Alyssa: Four and four are eight, so four and three make seven.

Children's ease with this problem encouraged us to ask them to try to show their thinking on paper, even though it was quite early in the school year. While some got very involved in trying to draw the storyboard, and others didn't have much of a clue, about two-thirds of our first graders were able to respond to the problem in some kind of written form.

Michael proudly presented his work showing seven kids. When asked how many had gotten off, he said that seven were on the bus, which indicated

40

that he had some understanding of what was going on, even though he wasn't actually able to solve the problem.

Angelique said she put four beans behind the door on her storyboard and then counted the kids on the bus and that made seven. She showed her work by writing the numbers four, five, six, seven.

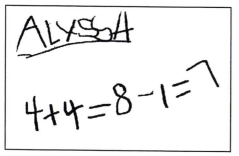

Brian proudly drew the appropriate number of kids in both places but since English is his second language, he pointed to two friends and indicated that they helped him.

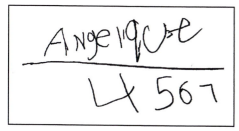

While the number sentence Alyssa wrote was not as straightforward as one an adult might have written, her work indicated a sophisticated understanding of number relationships more typical of older children. When we asked our second graders to respond to one anothers' School Bus Kids story problems in writing, many used pictures and numbers, but were more likely than our first graders to accompany their work with some written words of explanation as well.

Plan to go through three or four student problems in the first sharing session. When children call out answers (as many of our first graders do), encourage them to explain how they arrived at their solutions. While it's important to acknowledge each child's story problem, it's difficult to get through every piece in two or even three class sharing sessions. We suggest you post the remaining story problems in a prominent location in your classroom to admire and read over a few days' time with your class. When you're finished with the entire collection, consider saving children's problems, along with their written responses, in individual math portfolios for future assessment purposes.

NOTES

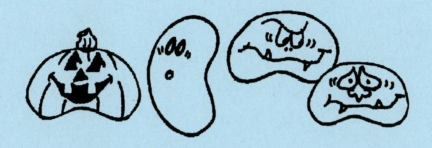

Pumpkins,
Goblins & Ghosts

Pumpkins, Goblins & Ghosts

T his theme is divided into two parts: Patterns and Trick or Treat. Part I, Patterns, is a departure from the computation story problems featured in School Bus Kids. Rather than asking children to figure out how many in all, how many are left, or how many for each, we invite them to look at a pictorial pattern we've created and ascertain what's behind the secret door by analyzing the parts of the pattern they can see. In these problems, just as in so many of the computation situations we pose, students must look at all the available information to arrive at a solution.

As before, we pose the first problems and then encourage students to create their own. This process takes about a week. At the easiest level, children build patterns with lima bean counters painted to look like pumpkins, goblins, and ghosts. They choose a favorite pattern to replicate on paper with tiny cut-outs and tape a secret door over a segment of their work. Later, classmates try to figure out what's hidden.

At a somewhat more difficult level, children reproduce linear patterns they've created on 3 x 3, 4 x 4, or even 5 x 5 grids; they place secret doors strategically, hiding a part of the pattern, to challenge their classmates.

The completed fence patterns and/or pattern grids are bound into class books to be figured out during whole group instruction, then added to the class library or set out as an additional pattern activity for independent investigation.

The most complex problems in Part I challenge children to create patterns with a set number of counters, determined by a double spinner. A student may, for example, be challenged to build a repeating pattern with eight pumpkins, four ghosts, and two goblins. He or she must use all the counters, but can create a pattern that breaks off midstream.

The problems in Part II, Trick or Treat, revisit every whole number operation introduced in the School Bus Kids theme. This time, however, addition subtraction, multiplication, and division stories center around Halloween as pumpkins, ghosts, and goblins wink from windows, float over fences, or hide behind the doors of haunted houses. As before, it takes a week or more to pose problems, examine problem models with the class, and have students create and share their own story problems.

Note: If you don't choose to implement a Halloween theme in your classroom, please see Theme 2B for an alternate set of problems and problem models based on things that go bump in the night and lurk at the foot of every child's bed. Night Critters is non-holiday based, and has created, in our classrooms, much the same magic as Pumpkins, Goblins, and Ghosts.

On Halloween, a trick-or-treater saw 10 ghosts, 12 goblins, and 4 pumpkins. How many eyes?

Part I: Patterning

When we first introduced Pumpkins, Goblins, and Ghosts in early October we intended to work with whole number operations, but our students had different ideas. Their joy in creating patterns with these bean characters led us to encourage them to craft Halloween pattern problems for their class-mates. The linear patterns with their randomly placed secret doors proved to be absolutely magical.

As we watched our first graders work, we wondered how to extend the challenge to seven- and eight-year-olds and decided to introduce grids. Could students move linear patterns onto grids and add secret doors? All of our second graders could and many first graders rose to the challenge as well. We had to chuckle when the combined magic of secret doors and scotch tape caused a few youngsters to apply so many doors that their problems became impossible to solve. Their peers let them know in a hurry that they had to be able to see more parts of the pattern in order to figure out what was hidden. Off they went to remove a few of their cherished doors.

Although the grid patterns challenged many of our students, we wanted to be sure we were posing real problems to even the most talented. We began by posting specified quantities of counters: three pumpkins, two ghosts, and two goblins, for instance. Could children create a repeating pattern that would use all the prescribed characters?

To make the activity a bit more fun, we added spinners to determine the numbers of pumpkins, goblins, and ghosts children would use to create their own patterns. Spinners, we knew, could be duplicated and put together by our students at minimal expense and could even go home with sets of paper pumpkins, goblins, and ghosts for family math. In the end, we felt Spinner Patterns was an extremely flexible and valuable activity for second grade.

45

SECRET DOOR LINEAR PATTERNS

You will need...

- overhead of fence storyboard, Blackline B19
- overhead pumpkins, goblins, and ghosts, 5 of each, Blackline B1
- Secret Door Linear Pattern problem models 1 & 2, Blacklines B21-B22
- pumpkin, goblin, and ghost counters, p. 184
- 6" x 12" black construction paper for pattern backgrounds, 30 or more
- 3" x 12" light brown construction paper for fences, 30 or more
- precut paper lima bean shapes in orange, green, and white, about 150 of each, p. 191; Blackline B2
- 2" x 3" black construction paper for secret doors, 30 or more
- ultra-fine Sanford Sharpies (must be used in an area away from the glue)
- glue and scotch tape to share

Begin the lesson by showing your fence overhead and a few overhead pumpkins, goblins, and ghosts. (If you don't have an overhead, use your lima bean characters on a paper fence board to demonstrate.) Challenge children to figure out how to pattern the Halloween critters along the top of the fence.

Once the pattern is complete, cover a portion of it with a secret door (a 2" x 3" piece of black construction paper). Can the children figure out which characters are hidden under the door by studying the rest of the pattern? Demonstrate placing the door in different spots, including the very beginning.

Next, show the students the problem models you've prepared for this activity and challenge them to figure out what's behind the secret door in each example. Finally, show them the materials they can use to create their own Secret Door Linear Patterns. Remind children to set up their patterns with the bean characters first.

After they get friends to check whether their patterns are really patterns, they should get matching paper lima bean shapes and pens to draw faces. Be

sure to point out that the pens will be ruined by coming in contact with glue and must be used carefully. Once all the faces are drawn on their paper bean characters, students can create fence backgrounds for their patterns, glue down their characters and, finally, tape on secret doors.

We like to use the children's Secret Door Linear Patterns for class problem solving. You might have children take turns presenting their pattern problems to the class to solve. Another thing you might try is binding students'

problems into small books of six or seven to challenge the class. As children work to solve one anothers' problems, consider asking them to draw their solutions on paper. This is a non-threatening first step toward illustrating their thinking in more difficult problems later.

When this activity has run its course, put the small books out in a tub for independent student use or onto the class library shelves. Many of our students choose to put secret door linear patterns into their math portfolios and we add samples of their solutions to other children's pattern problems too.

SECRET DOOR GRID PATTERNS

You will need...
- 3 x 3, 4 x 4, and 5 x 5 overhead grids, Blacklines B25-B27
- overhead pumpkins, goblins, and ghosts, Blackline B1
- Secret Door Grid Pattern problem models 1, 2, & 3, Blacklines B22-B24
- pumpkin, goblin, and ghost beans, p. 184
- 3 x 3, 4 x 4, and 5 x 5 grids, 30 or more copies of each, Blacklines B25-B27
- 1½" x 1½" black construction paper for secret doors, 150 pieces
- precut paper lima bean shapes in orange, green, and white, 100+;
  Blackline B2
- ultra-fine Sanford Sharpies to share
- glue and scotch tape to share

Begin the lesson by showing your overhead of one of the grids and a few

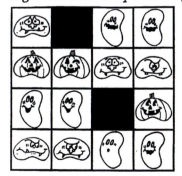

overhead pumpkins, goblins, and ghosts. (If you don't have an overhead, use your lima bean characters on a paper grid to demonstrate.) Challenge students to figure out how to pattern the Halloween critters in linear fashion. Once the pattern is complete, move it to the grid and cover one character with a secret door. Can the children figure out which critter is hidden under the door by studying the rest of the pattern? What would happen if there were two doors? three?

Next, show the students the problem models you've prepared for this activity and challenge them to figure out what's behind the secret doors in each example. Finally, show them the materials they can use to create their own Secret Door Grid Patterns, which will probably be at least as interesting and challenging as yours.

Remind children to set up their patterns with the bean characters first. After they get friends to make sure their patterns really work, they should get matching paper lima bean shapes and pens to draw faces. (Be sure to point out that they must use the pens before gluing.)

When all their paper bean characters have faces, students can glue their patterns to grids and tape on secret doors. Three by three grids are easiest to work with at first, but we find that children seem to challenge themselves at appropriate levels if we set out all the grids (3 x 3, 4 x 4, and 5 x 5) and let them choose.

We also try to provide students with more than one opportunity to do this activity; as soon as they see how easy the 3 x 3 grid problems are for their classmates to solve, they want to create more challenging puzzles.

We like to use the children's Secret Door Grid Patterns for class problem solving. You might have children take turns presenting their pattern problems for the class to solve or, to challenge the class, you might bind students' problems into small books of six or seven. As children work to solve one anothers' problems, consider asking them to draw their solutions on paper. This is a non-threatening first step toward illustrating their thinking in more difficult problems later.

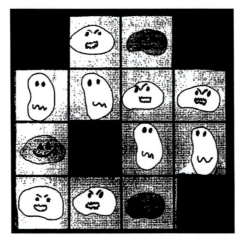

When this activity has run its course, put the small books out in a tub for independent student use or onto the class library shelves. Many of our students choose to put secret door grid patterns into their math portfolios and we add samples of their solutions to other children's pattern problems too.

SPINNER PATTERNS ✪

You will need...

- a Spinner Patterns double spinner, made ahead (See Blackline B28 for spinner tops and directions for spinner assembly.)
- pumpkin, goblin, and ghost beans
- Spinner Patterns spinner tops, 1 copy per student, Blackline B28
- Spinner Patterns record sheet, 1 copy per student, Blackline B29
- brass fasteners, 2 per student
- regular size paper clips, 2 per student
- tiny lengths of a narrow drinking straw (the straws many schools give out at lunch are perfect), 2 per student
- a 6" x 11" piece of poster board or heavy oak tag, 1 per student
- glue to share

Begin the lesson by using your double spinner and lima bean counters to go through the entire activity with the students' help.

Teacher: Let's spin the spinners and see what we get.

Children: This looks like fun. Those spinners are neat! They've got numbers on one wheel and ghosts, goblins, and pumpkins on the other side. Are we going to use them to make patterns?

Teacher: Yes, we're going to let the spinners dictate how many of each kind we'll have to use to form a repeating pattern.

Children: How many times do we get to spin?

Teacher: Let's experiment and see what happens. How about if we try just two spins of each wheel the first time? We'll have to record the number and kind we get from each spin.

Children: Four...goblins! Spin again.

Teacher: Let's write that on the chalkboard so we don't forget.

Children: What if we get more goblins?

Teacher: What do you think we should do?

Children: We could add them to the others. We could just say you have to spin again.

Teacher: I'll leave it to you to make those decisions once you make your own spinners. Let's try another spin and see what happens.

Children: Five pumpkins! That's easy! If you had four goblins and five pumpkins, you could just go ABABABABA.

Teacher: Is that the only kind of pattern you could make with four goblins and five pumpkins?

Lonson: We could do AABBAABBA.

Billie Ray: Or ABBA, ABBA, A...

Teacher: You're very good at that. Let's try more spins and see what happens.

Children: Let's do five spins this time and we'll write them down and then add them up.

Teacher: That sounds quite challenging but let's give it a try. I need someone to record our spins on the board. (Teacher spins the double spinner five times while a student records the results of each spin on the chalkboard.)

2 pumpkins, 4 pumpkins, 3 goblins, 5 ghosts, and 4 pumpkins

Children: Oh, no. That's ten pumpkins, five ghosts, and three goblins. That's going to be hard. We need some of those beans. Can I use Unifix cubes instead? I want to draw it. I'm going to write P for pumpkin, a big G for goblin, and a small g for ghost and write it out.

Teacher: You have lots of good ideas. Let's get started.

Once children understand the nature of this game, show them how to make their own double spinners (you'll find instructions printed directly on the spinner blackline). When they're ready, provide pumpkin, goblin, and ghost lima bean counters and Spinner Patterns record sheets. Some children may find five spins are too many, while others will want to do more. In any event, they'll spin at least twice (and no more than nine times), record the results on their record sheets, and then work with the pumpkin, goblin, and ghost beans to solve the problems they create (see example). We encourage children to show their solutions with bean-shaped blobs of color or letters rather than carefully drawn characters.

Children who especially enjoy the Spinner Pattern challenges can take home their double spinners, self-designed paper pumpkins, goblins, and

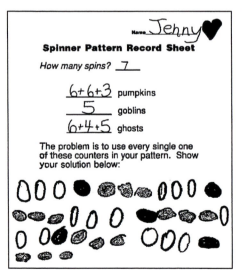

ghosts, and a few record sheets to use for family math.

You might also want to save samples of children's record sheets—false starts and successes—for assessment purposes. When you collect assorted samples of problem solving over several months, definite trends begin to emerge in each child's collections. You'll also get a chance to celebrate your own teaching efforts when you see the wide variety of tactics your children use in solving problems.

II: **Trick or Treat**

Getting Started

When we returned to computational problem solving in Trick or Treat, things went much more smoothly than in September. The children found it somewhat easier to explain their strategies and displayed growing confidence throughout all phases of their work. The problems they created for one another, first graders with pictures only, second graders with pictures and words, seemed indicative of their comfort level with various operations. All in all, we were feeling a lot more confident about using the story boxes to provide challenging problems for our children to solve. Our hard work in September was already beginning to pay off.

ADDITION, SUBTRACTION, MULTIPLICATION & DIVISION

You will need...
- overhead of Pumpkins, Goblins & Ghosts storyboard, Blackline B30
- overhead pumpkins, goblins, and ghosts, 8 of each, Blackline B1
- Pumpkins, Goblins & Ghosts storyboard, 1 copy per student, Blackline B30
- storybox counters, 8 pumpkins, 8 goblins, and 8 ghosts per student, p.184

Begin the new theme by posing the problems below. Ask children to work with their storyboards and lima bean characters to set up and solve the problems, but don't insist on the use of these manipulatives by all students if some are able to work mentally at times. (This is more likely to occur among second graders than first.) As your students solve the problems, encourage them to share their different strategies with the group. It will probably take two class sessions, possibly longer, to cover this set of problems. Second grade teachers may want to skip a few of the very easiest examples and emphasize the starred problems.

How Many Altogether?

● The little boy noticed four giggling ghosts beside the door. Five green goblins were peeking through the windows. How many Halloween creatures did he see?

✪ The three upstairs windows were full of ghosts—two in each window. The door was blocked by seven goblins. How many ghosts and goblins were visiting the haunted house?

Adding Three or More Numbers

● A trick-or-treater saw three ghosts peeking from the attic windows, one goblin lurking beside the door, and four pumpkins sitting on the fence. How many Halloween creatures did he see in all?

● The trick-or-treater saw two pumpkins in the attic window, six beside the door, and two sitting on the fence. How many pumpkins did she see altogether?

✪ The old house was nearly ready for the neighborhood block party. The flickering candlelight of two pumpkins in each of the upstairs windows cast enough light toward the fence that the eight ghosts the children had made were quite an eerie sight. Three green goblins sat in front of the old door. How many Halloween critters in all?

How Many Are Left?

● There were seven pumpkins lined up by the old house door. Suddenly the door opened, hurtling three of them completely away. How many were left?

✪ There were twelve pumpkins, goblins, and ghosts sitting altogether along the old fence. Suddenly, a trick-or-treater threw the pillow case he was carrying over four of them. How many were still visible?

Missing Addend / Missing Subtrahend

● A little girl dressed as Red Riding Hood passed by and saw seven ghosts floating above the fence. She was determined to catch some. She quickly took off her red cape and threw it over some of the ghosts, leaving only three still visible. How many did she catch?

● As the young trick-or-treater walked by, he noticed seven green goblins frolicking above the fence. He took off the sheet he was wearing and threw it over some of them. When he ran off, there were only two left above the fence. How many did he capture?

52

✪ The young girl was quite sure there were eleven Halloween critters in the haunted house, but she could only see three in the windows. How many were behind the door?

✪ One of the trick-or-treaters pulled off his Dracula cape and threw it over four Halloween critters on the fence. He could still see seven more Halloween critters. How many creatures were on the fence before he captured the four?

. . . .

Comparing or Finding The Difference

● The trick or-treater saw three ghosts hovering above the fence and two goblins slinking around the base of the fence. How many more ghosts than goblins did he see?

● The little boy saw six pumpkins sitting on the fence and three ghosts hovering above the fence. How many more pumpkins than ghosts did he see?

. . . .

Twice As Many / Multiplication

● There were four Halloween creatures hovering above the fence one evening, and twice that many hiding behind the door of the haunted house. How many were behind the door? How many in all?

● The trick-or-treater saw four pumpkins in each of the two attic windows. How many pumpkins in all?

✪ While he was out trick-or-treating, a little boy saw four grinning jack-o'-lanterns on the fence. Twice as many goblins were slinking along the ground. How many more goblins than jack-o'-lanterns did he see?

✪ Seven green goblins peered out of the attic window at the trick-or-treaters standing below. How many goblins' eyes were visible?

. . . .

Half As Many / Division

● There were four goofy goblins skipping around the attic of the haunted house and half as many hidden behind the door. How many were behind the door? How many were in the house altogether?

● The little girl saw eight Halloween creatures on the fence and half that many sitting by the door of the haunted house. How many were beside the door? How many creatures did she see in all?

✪ As the trick-or-treater passed by the haunted house, he noticed fourteen bright eyes gleaming at him from the windows. Can you show how many pumpkins there must have been?

✪ The families in the neighborhood were decorating the big house for Halloween. One family brought twelve pumpkins to display. The children decided they wanted each upstairs window to have an equal number of pumpkins. How many should they put in each upstairs window?

Creating Story Problems

In October, we present models of story problems in both pictures and words (problem models), which children examine and then solve. After working with our examples, children go on to create their own story problems. Some copy or modify our ideas only slightly, while others are able to invent their own pictorial, written, or mathematical twists. Although nearly all second graders can be expected to write stories to accompany their picture problems at this point, most first graders will be far more comfortable posing story problems in picture form only.

EXAMINING SOME POSSIBILITIES

You will need...
- Trick or Treat problem models, Blacklines B31-B44
- Pumpkins, Goblins, & Ghosts storyboard, 1 copy per student, Blackline B30
- pumpkins, goblins, and ghosts, 8 of each per student

Note: If you are a second grade teacher, consider omitting one or two of the very easiest models and featuring the two that are starred. You'll notice that our problem models aren't as challenging as some of the examples in the Getting Started section. This is because they're meant to help children write their own story problems. We find that most primary students aren't able to pose problems at quite the level they can solve them. Your more capable second graders may find their own ways to "jazz up" the easier models, however. If you are a first grade teacher, you'll probably want to limit your choice of problem models to five or six; more than that may prove overwhelming when children try to choose models on which to base their own problems.

Begin by asking children to examine the picture portion of one of your problem models. Can they figure out what the problem is by looking at the picture alone? Show them the written story problem on the flap. Does the story help to clarify the problem to be solved?

First Grade Teacher: I've put together some new problem models for you to solve today. Although the written story problem is hidden in each, I'm eager to see if you can tell what the problem is simply by looking at the

picture. What do you notice about the first example here?

Children: There are four ghosts in the window and three pumpkins on the fence. No, wait—there are four pumpkins because there's one in front of the door. Maybe that one pumpkin wants to get into the house.

Teacher: Have a look at the question mark in this picture. The artist has used question marks to signal what it is she wants us to figure out in her picture problems.

Children: The little kid has a question mark over his head. Maybe he's wondering if it's safe to go into that spooky house. Or maybe he's asking the pumpkin by the door if it wants to come over to the fence.

Clara: Oh, I know! Remember the school bus problems we saw? When someone is thinking that question mark, it means they want us to add all the things together.

Ryan: But it could mean something different this time.

Mason: Like maybe the pumpkin by the door is going to go inside—and the kid is wondering how many will be left.

Raissa: That's easy! Three!

David: But look, there's a word under the question mark. It says "altogether". The whole thing says, "How many altogether?"

Children: All we have to do is add up those ghosts and pumpkins? That's easy—it's seven! See? One, two, three, four, five, six, seven.

Kim: Don't forget about the pumpkin by the door. It's really like four and four—it makes eight!

Teacher: This seems like an easy one to solve, once you figure out what the problem is. Let's fold down the flap at the bottom of the page and read the story that goes along with the picture to see if there's a match between your thinking and the written part of the problem (see next page).

Children: It is adding. I knew it! So did I!

Have students examine each of your problem models, discussing, reading, and solving the problems as they go. We find that some children are able to solve our picture/word problems mentally in the process of examining them, but they can certainly use the pumpkins, goblins, ghosts, and storyboards if they need them. In some cases, the real challenge to youngsters may lie in "reading the pictures" to figure out what's being asked. This is not to be overlooked or solved by simply reading the text on the story flap, because you'll be asking your first and second graders alike to frame their own problems pictorially too. The only way most children can handle this initially is to imitate the pictures and symbols you provide, but eventually the question mark comes to stand for the difference between a story and a story problem: a shorthand symbol that facilitates children's thinking as they learn to pose problems.

Once all your problem models have been examined, display them in a prominent area at eye level so students can think about which ones they might like to copy or modify when they create their own story problems.

TRICK OR TREAT PROBLEM MODELS

To make copies of these problem models for use in your own classroom, see Blacklines B31-B44.

Problem Model 1

The boy saw four ghosts in the window, one pumpkin in front of the door and three pumpkins on the fence. How many in all?

TRICK OR TREAT PROBLEM MODELS (CONT.)

**Problem
Model 2**

The girl was sure she'd seen six pumpkins in the
haunted house but when she looked again, there
were only four. How many were hiding behind
the door?

**Problem
Model 3**

A trick-or-treater dressed up as a ghost saw
seven goblins floating above the fence. He threw
his sheet over some to capture them. He missed
three. How many did he catch?

TRICK OR TREAT PROBLEM MODELS (CONT.)

Problem Model 4

The girl saw five pumpkins on the fence and three ghosts floating above the fence. How many more pumpkins than ghosts did she see?

Problem Model 5

There were six creatures in the windows of the haunted house and half as many hiding behind the door. How many were behind the door?

TRICK OR TREAT PROBLEM MODELS (CONT.)

**Problem
Model 6**

The night before Halloween, there were six
pumpkins in the windows of the haunted house.
On Halloween, someone had carved two eyes in
each. How many eyes altogether?

✪
**Problem
Model 7**

✪ The trick-or-treater saw three pumpkins in
each of the attic windows. How many pumpkins
altogether?

TRICK OR TREAT PROBLEM MODELS (CONT.)

✪
**Problem
Model 8**

✪ **The young ghost with his trick or treat bag
saw fourteen eyes peeking down at him from the
haunted house. How many creatures were in the
house?**

Crafting Story Problems

When all the problem models have been examined and solved, display them
where children can easily refer to each kind as they create their own problems for others to solve. This early in the school year, you'll find that many
students will copy your models almost exactly, changing only the numbers.

Other students, particularly second graders, may begin to modify your
ideas or insert their own unique twists, especially if you encourage them to
create problems that will interest and challenge their classmates. October
was the month one of our very gifted second graders decided to pose problems for the kids by writing his number words in German. Another one of
our students combined two of the problem models to create a real stumper:

> On Halloween, a trick-or-treater saw 10 ghosts, 12 goblins, and 4 pumpkins.
> How many eyes?

You will need...

- 9" x 12" black construction paper, 1 sheet per student, *or* the Pumpkins,
  Goblins, & Ghosts storyboard, Blackline B30, 1 copy per student (see Note
  below)

- 3" x 4" black construction paper for house doorways

- assorted cut pieces of construction paper for trick-or-treaters

- white construction paper in various sizes to make "talking bubbles" for question marks, word, and numbers the signal the problems to be solved
- precut construction paper bean shapes in orange, green, and white for pumpkins, goblins, and ghosts, about 150 of each color, p. 191
- 4" x 9" brown construction paper for fences*
- haunted house blackline, copies for children to cut out and use if they desire*
- crayons, scissors, glue, and marking pens to share
- ultra-fine Sanford sharpie pens to share

  additional materials for second graders:
- 4½" x 12" black construction paper for story flaps, 1 per student*
- student writing paper and pencils

Note: Before you gather the materials to have your children create their own story problems, think about whether you want them to start from scratch, using black construction paper backgrounds, or whether you want them to start with blackline copies of the Pumpkins, Goblins, and Ghosts storyboard. Starting with blackline copies of the storyboard is somewhat easier in that children have only to color in the fences and haunted houses and add bean characters and trick-or-treaters, but starting from scratch produces more charming results. Matthew, whose work is shown below, started with black construction paper. He used a copy of our haunted house and precut bean shapes, but created his own fence and trick-or-treater. If you decide to have students create their story problems from scratch, you'll need the items marked with asterisks (*) above, in addition to the other materials listed.

Explain that you want each child to prepare a Halloween story problem for the rest of the class. It is important that the picture portion pose the problem as clearly as possible and, for second graders, that the written portion support the picture with all needed details. Most second graders will want to begin with the picture part of their problems and may need another day before they're able to finish the written part. You may want to set some limits on the numbers children can use in their own problems, too. We asked our first graders to work with twelve or fewer bean characters; the limit for second grade was twenty-six.

When children's story problems are complete, encourage them to check with classmates to see if their work makes sense. Can other children understand what needs to be solved? Have they posed problems that can be solved by peers? Finally, have youngsters meet with you for final conferencing or editing as needed. Some first graders may need to explain their thinking to you and may even want to dictate a written portion. Second graders may need to refine a question or clarify their story in some way.

Second grade teachers will need to type or print each child's problem on a 3½" x 11" strip of white paper, using standard spelling and punctuation. Since we both have Macintosh computers, we like to use a bold 36-point font with a sideways page setup. That way, we can type the whole batch of story problems at once, print them out and cut them apart. Most computers have at least a 24-point font. If you don't have access to a computer, you can print children's problems with a regular tip Sanford Sharpie. The point is to wind up with good quality print large enough to be read at a distance.

The next day, have children tape these story flaps along the bottom of their story problem pictures. If they've worked from scratch using construction paper instead of blackline copies of the storyboard to create their story problems, they'll need to glue the typed or printed strips to the 4½" x 12" strips of construction paper you precut in preparation for this activity, and

A boy saw 2 pumpkins in the attic and 2 pumpkins in the lattice window, 2 ghosts in the lattice window and 2 goblins in the windows and 2 goblins by the grave and 2 pumpkins by the grave. How many altogether?

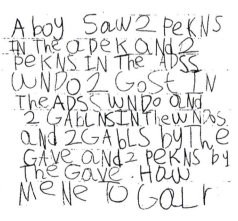

then tape the flaps to their pictures along the bottom on the back side. Also, have each child glue the draft copy of his or her writing to the back of his or her picture. Incorporating the rough draft into a finished product validates children's hard work and can be a nice source of information about students' growing capabilities in the areas of writing and spelling.

Solving Student Problems

Once children have completed their own story problems, it's sharing time. This is a time when many children begin to develop a sense of audience. For this reason, we try to feature every story, if not during a whole-group sharing session, then in a class book or wall display, or as part of a homework assignment. We usually select four or five particularly interesting or unique problems for initial presentation to the group, however. As in September, the children are seated on the rug with writing materials and easy access to the storyboards and bean characters.

As they work through each problem, ask students to explain the various ways they are finding solutions and then encourage them to record their thinking via illustrations, numbers, and/or words. Many students will be delighted to use the beans and storyboards or their fingers as they solve problems, and will then draw pictures to show what they've done; others may disregard the available manipulatives and start with sketches or written number sentences. Written solutions will still be somewhat rudimentary this early in the year, but if youngsters are able to record their thinking in any form, be sure to tuck it into portfolios for future assessment purposes.

You will need...

- student problems, select 4 or 5
- half sheets of ditto paper and pencils, along with hard writing surfaces (clipboards or student chalkboards are fine)
- Pumpkins, Goblins, and Ghosts storyboards and bean characters for children to share as needed
- an overhead transparency of the Pumpkins, Goblins, and Ghosts storyboard, along with overhead counters if you want children to be able to demonstrate their strategies to one another

Present one problem at a time (or have the student author present it), allow time for questions or clarification, and have children spend some time working on their own at the rug. Expect some amount of interchange among students, especially first graders, and plenty of looking around and imitation on the part of those who don't quite understand. After a few minutes, ask those who are willing to share their solutions and explain their strategies.

First Grade Teacher: What do you notice about Kristen's problem?

Children: That's good. She wrote something. I can read it. Not me! It says "How many more?" She even put a goblin with the part she wrote. What does she mean? I see some ghosts and some goblins. I bet she wants to know how many more goblins there are. They're not the same. She put on a lot of goblins and ghosts.

Cory: But she wants to know how many more goblins than ghosts.

Ginny: I can't do it. It's too hard.

Brandon: I can. It's seven. That's how many goblins she made.

Jessica: But that doesn't tell how many more. That's just counting the goblins.

Cory: Here. I drew the beans. I think you have to figure out how many are the same and then count the other kind. I put a ghost  touching a goblin. Then a ghost touching a goblin. Then a ghost touching a goblin—see. Here are the ones that can't touch.

Andrew: I wrote it. I wrote the lines like on the calendar—the kind in fives and when we circle the tens. These are the lines for the goblins. These are the lines for the ghosts. I didn't make any diagonal lines. Then I put a ring around where they were both the same.

Ginny: I still don't get it. This is too hard.

Teacher: Would anyone like to show us on the overhead how you figured it out? There are children who are feeling quite confused about what it is we're trying to figure out.

Jessica: I think I can. It's like the graphs we did in kindergarten and our Teddy Bear Graph we did when we showed how some of our teddy bears

were wearing clothes and some weren't wearing clothes. I remember there were more without any clothes. See. I think you put them in rows like this. These two are the same. These are the same. These are the same. See. But these goblins are extras. There are four more goblins.

Teacher: We're seeing some great solutions. Did anyone figure it out another way?

Justin: I used my fingers. I just counted. I got ten altogether.

The "How many more?" problem Kristen has posed to her classmates isn't accessible at this time to every child. With additional time and future opportunities however, nearly every child will understand this kind of problem and find ways to solve it.

Teacher: Let's try a different kind. Here's a trick-or-treater who seems quite perplexed. What do you think we have to figure out?

Children: It says, "seven" above the ghost's head. I think there must be some inside that door. I can do that one. Me, too. I can figure it out.

Kyrie: I think there are two behind the door.

Kylie: The kid thinks some are hiding in the door. I can see some because the door is open a tiny bit.

Children: It's like with the school bus kids when the driver was trying to figure out the ones behind the door. You have to count the ones you can see and then use your fingers to figure it out. Not me. I just count and then put some beans behind the door. Not me. I wrote the numbers on my paper to figure it out. I drew it on my paper.

Plan to go through five or six student problems in the first sharing session. If you've encouraged your students to record their solutions on paper, you'll probably want to save them to get a sense of the various strategies your entire group is using to solve different kinds of problems and also to examine individuals' current strengths and areas of need.

While you'll want to acknowledge every child's work, it's not usually practical to try to do more than two or three class sharing sessions. We've listed some of the other ways we honor each problem:

• Post the entire collection on one of your classroom walls after the first few have been shared with the class. Admire and solve a few each day with your whole class. (We believe it's important to provide a "print-rich" classroom environment so we often "read the walls" with our children.)

• Bind the story problems into mini-books to be enjoyed during math or reading time.

• Share some of the collection with another class for them to work.

• Send reduced copies of some as homework over a two to three week time span. (We include a note with the homework that tells parents they can look forward to seeing work from *every* class member over the next few months. We know, as parents, we look for our own child's problem first.)

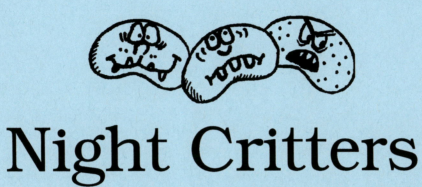

Night Critters

Theme 2B

Night Critters

F or teachers who don't choose to implement Halloween-related activities in their classrooms but like the appeal of imaginary creatures, we've included a variation on the theme: Night Critters. In this section, you'll find problems based on the comings and goings of things that go bump in the night and lurk at the foot of every child's bed. Although the problems and problem models are different, the routines for teaching Night Critters are nearly identical to Pumpkins, Goblins, and Ghosts. We ask you to refer to pages 51-66, in addition to the notes below, for instructions and insights.

To make alternate storyboards, counters, and problem models, please see Preparation of Materials. Should you decide to pursue Night Critters, you might want to read a few monster-type books to your students before you start posing problems. Some of the books currently available address children's nighttime fears in a very sincere but humorous fashion, while others are purely fanciful. All serve to set the stage for wonderful story (problem) telling. Here are a few of our personal favorites:

There's a Nightmare in My Closet by Mercer Mayer (1985)
There's a Monster Under My Bed by James Howe (1990)
Clyde Monster by Robert L. Crowe (1986)
A World Full of Monsters by John Troy McQueen (1986)
Harry and the Terrible Whatzit by Dick Gackenback (1984)
After-School Monster by Marissa Moss (1991)
Maggie and the Monster by Elizabeth Winthrop (1987)

67

Getting Started

ADDITION, SUBTRACTION, MULTIPLICATION & DIVISION

You will need...

• overhead of Night Critters storyboard, Blackline B47

• overhead night critters, 8 of each color, Blackline B1

• Night Critters storyboard, 1 copy per student, Blackline B47

• night critters, 8 of each color per student, p. 185

Begin this theme by posing the problems below and asking children to work with their storyboards and night critter characters. As your students solve the problems, encourage them to share the different strategies they're using. It will probably take two class sessions or more to cover this set of problems. Second grade teachers may want to emphasize the starred problems. For additional teaching tips and insights, please read Pumpkins, Goblins, and Ghosts, Getting Started, pages 51-54.

....

How Many Altogether?

● Just before bed, the little boy had watched a scary television show. Now his imagination was running wild. He peered out from under his pillow and was sure he saw four dreadful night critters oozing out of his closet door. Then he saw five more slinking around at the foot of his bed. How many critters did he see in all?

....

Adding Three or More Numbers

✪ Had she forgotten to close her closet door? The little girl was certain she could see it opening. Oh, no! There were five night critters creeping out of the door. They seemed to be looking for their friends. Were there more in the room? She looked around and saw four of the rotten rascals by the foot of her bed. Five more were floating above her head. How many critters had entered her room?

....

How Many Are Left?

● There were seven slimy critters lurking behind the closet door. Five of them were lonely and wanted to be near a child. They crept noiselessly out of the closet and into the sleeping boy's room. How many were left in the closet?

....

Missing Addend / Missing Subtrahend

● Was it just a bad dream or were there some night critters fluttering around the room? The little boy woke up his older brother to help him look. At first, they were sure they saw nine of the scoundrels but when they looked again, only three of them were still in the room. Apparently, the others had slipped into the closet. How many were in the closet?

✪ Could it be! Did the sisters see the closet door open? Five, ten, fifteen! Fifteen of the night critters seemed to be floating into their room. Mom, Dad! When Mom and Dad came in, they could see only seven. Possibly the rest had drifted back into the closet. How many were in the closet?

....

Comparing or Finding The Difference

● The closet seemed to be opening. The boy sat up to look. He could see five night critters peeking out from behind the door and three sitting at the foot of his bed. How many more were coming out of the door than were sitting on the foot of his bed?

✪ The neighborhood friends were having a slumber party and they'd been telling scary stories. Suddenly, one of the children said she could see eleven night critters above the bed. Another child said there were four under the bed. How many fewer were under the bed than above the bed?

....

Twice As Many

● There were three gruesome night critters under the bed and twice as many above the bed. How many critters were above the bed? How many were in the room altogether?

✪ There were six scary night critters floating around the room. Twice as many lurked in the closet. How many were in the closet? How many were in the room altogether?

....

Half As Many

● There were eight ghastly night critters drifting around the room and half as many hiding in the closet. How many were in the closet? How many altogether?

✪ Was it all that popcorn? Maybe it was too many sodas. Or, maybe it was that movie. Whatever it was, the teenager was having a hard time sleeping. It seemed that his room was filling with night critters. First he thought he saw twelve over his bed. Then he began to believe there were half that many under his bed. How many were under the bed? How many were in the room altogether?

Division: Sharing / Grouping

● The small girl heard some strange sounds. She peeked out from under her quilt and thought she saw eight eyes peering down at her. How many night critters were above her bed?

✪ It couldn't be! It was! How terrible! There were eighteen eyes peering down at the young child. How many night critters were in the room?

Creating Story Problems

Once children have had an opportunity to work though a substantial number of the problems above, present models of story problems in picture and word form for students to examine and solve. After working with your models, have children create their own problems.

EXAMINING SOME POSSIBILITIES

You will need...

• Night Critters problem models, Blacklines B48-B59

• Night Critters storyboard, Blackline B47

• night critters, 8 each of 2 colors per student, p. 185

Begin by asking children to examine the picture portion of one of your problem models. Can they figure out what the problem is by looking at the picture alone? Show them the written story problem on the flap. Does the story help to clarify the problem to be solved?

Second Grade Teacher: I've brought in some illustrated night critter problems today. Have a look at this one—what do you think the problem is here?

Children: There are six monsters floating around over the girl's head. Maybe there are more in the closet? Does that door open?

Teacher: Nope. Do you see any other clues?

Shalonda: There's a bubble over her head. It says, "Six monsters...question mark...eyes."

Autumn: That probably means six monsters—how many eyes? Easy, just count!

Teacher: Okay, but before we do, let's look at the story flap to see if it has any more information we need.

Yikes! Their eyes glow in the dark! There are six of the miserable little things floating around my room. How many eyes?

Children: We were right! The problem is about eyes.

Have students examine each of your problem models, discussing, reading, and solving the problems as they go. We find that some children are able to solve our picture/word problems mentally in the process of examining them, but they can certainly use the night critters and storyboards if they need them. Once all your problem models have been examined, display them in a prominent area at eye level so students can think about which they might like to copy or modify when they create their own story problems.

NIGHT CRITTERS PROBLEM MODELS

To make copies of these problem models for use in your own classroom, see Blacklines B48-B59.

Problem Model 1

I think I hear them again. Good grief! Four are peeking out of the closet. Oh, no! Five are sitting on my bed. How many are there anyway?

NIGHT CRITTERS PROBLEM MODELS (CONT.)

**Problem
Model 2**

Not again! I think I must have forgotten to close my closet door. There are three of the varmints creeping out of my closet, four under my bed and two on my pillow. How many are in my room?

**Problem
Model 3**

I've had enough! I'll catch them. Two, four, six, eight! Eight of them. SMACK! How many did I get?

NIGHT CRITTERS PROBLEM MODELS (CONT.)

Problem Model 4

I hear them! They've got to be there. Oh no! Six are sitting on my bed and four are hiding under it. How many fewer are under the bed than on it?

Problem Model 5

Mom! Dad! Can I sleep in your room? My room is full of creepy little monsters. There are six hiding under my bed and I'm just sure there are half that many in the closet. How many are in the closet? How many altogether?

NIGHT CRITTERS PROBLEM MODELS (CONT.)

Problem Model 6

Yikes! Their eyes glow in the dark! There are six of the miserable little things floating around my room. How many eyes?

Problem Model 7

They really are filling up my room. Four of the critters have already oozed out of my closet and are floating over my head. I think there are twice as many in my closet. How many do you think are in there? How many critters altogether?

Crafting Story Problems

You will need...

- 9" x 12" black construction paper, 1 sheet per student, *or* Night Critters storyboard, 1 copy per student, Blackline B47 (see Note below)

- 3" x 5" pieces of brown construction paper for closet doors, 1 per student

- white construction paper in various sizes to make "talking bubbles" for question marks, words, and numbers that signal the problems to solved

- precut construction paper bean shapes in green and purple for night critters, about 150 of each color, Blackline B2

- Beds, Blackline 47, copies for children to cut out and use if they desire*

- crayons, scissors, glue, and marking pens to share

- ultra-fine Sanford Sharpie pens to share

  additional materials for second graders:

- 4¹⁄₂" black construction paper for story flaps, 1 per student*

- student writing paper and pencils

Note: Before you gather the materials to have your children create their own story problems, think about whether you want them to start from scratch, using black construction paper backgrounds, or whether you want them to start with blackline copies of the Night Critters storyboard. Starting from scratch produces very charming results, but the picture problems children create by starting with black-line copies of storyboards have their own appeal. The second grader who crafted the problem shown below started with a blackline copy of the critters board and a

There were 7 monsters in the boy's room. One of the monsters had 4 heads and the rest of them had one head. How many heads were in the room?

by Timmy

*precut closet door, but declined our offer of precut bean shapes, preferring to draw his own monsters. If you do decide to have students create their story problems from scratch, you'll need the items marked with asterisks (*) above, **in addition to** the other materials listed.*

To find out how to help children create their own picture/word story problems with these materials, please refer to Pumpkins, Goblins, and Ghosts, Crafting Story Problems, pages 60-63.

Solving Student Problems

You will need...

- student problems, select 4 or 5
- half sheets of ditto paper and pencils, along with hard writing surfaces (clipboards or student chalkboards are fine)
- Night Critters storyboards and bean characters for children to share as needed
- an overhead transparency of the Night Critters storyboards, along with overhead counters, if you want children to demonstrate their solutions for the entire group

Present one problem at a time (or have the student author present it), allow time for questions or clarification, and have children spend some time working on their own at the rug. Expect some interchange among students, especially first graders, and plenty of looking around and imitation by those who don't quite understand. After a few minutes, ask those who are willing to share their solutions and explain their strategies. Then encourage children to record their ideas on paper using pictures, numbers, and/or words.

Second Grade Teacher: What do you notice about JoDell's problem?

Children: There are four monsters in the kid's room. Two are on the bedposts and there are two floating around over her head. But the kid is

thinking nine. Maybe she's dreaming about nine. There must be some in the closet. Yeah—five!

Teacher: Let's have a look at JoDell's story flap to make sure that the problem really has to do with figuring out how many are in the closet. JoDell, would you like to read it to us?

JoDell: Sure!

There were 4 monsters flying around my bedroom. When I peeked out of my covers, I grabbed my flashlight and walked over to my closet. I knew that when I opened my closet door, there were going to be 9 monsters. How many monsters were in the closet?

Children: We were right. We do need to figure out how many in the closet.

Tanya: I already know it's five, because four plus five is nine. It has to be five.

Teacher: Tanya believes there are five critters in the closet. Does anyone have a different solution or a different way to figure it out?

Aaron: I think it's five too, but I counted on my fingers. I held four on one hand and kept counting until I got to nine. See? Four, five, six, seven, eight, nine. It took five more fingers to get to nine.

Kaylyn: I did the same thing with tally marks on my paper. I wrote down four and just kept going.

Timmy: I know it's five because you can see four, and four plus four plus one more is nine, and four plus one is five.

Children: Can we look under her closet door to see if we're right?

Teacher: Sure. After we've done that, I'd like you to record your thinking about JoDell's problem on paper. Try to use pictures, words, or numbers to show how you figured it out.

Plan to go through four or five student problems in the first sharing session, and for advice about how to acknowledge every student's work, please read Pumpkins, Goblins, and Ghosts, Solving Student Problems, page 63-66.

NOTES

Christmas Presents

Christmas Presents

T he lessons in this chapter run a course similar to the first two themes, but this time students work with miniature packages and parcels to solve problems posed orally and in written form. Addition, subtraction, multiplication, division, and partitioning stories center around Christmas as presents appear or disappear from the tree, the fireplace mantel, or the closet. Presents are also packaged in groups of ten (parcels), enabling teachers to extend students' thinking into the area of place value. As before, it takes a week or more to pose problems, examine problem models with your class, and have the students create and share their own story problems.

Note: After theme 3A, you'll find Theme 3B, a collection of problems and problem models based on a more generic Special Occasions theme should Christmas be a topic you don't wish to address. We advise you to read through the two themes and choose the problem set that best fits the needs of the students in your community.

HOW IT WORKED FOR US

After putting story boxes aside for the month of November, we found our students were quite eager to start a new theme. The magic of presents behind the closet door, in Santa's bag, under the tree, or even on the fireplace mantel intrigued nearly everyone. "Half as many" and "twice as many" didn't seem quite so mystifying to the first graders by December and our second graders enjoyed working in tens and ones as well as multiplying and dividing.

The new partitioning problems provided challenges for even our most capable seven- and eight-year olds:

> There were ten presents in the living room, two more under the tree than in front of the closet door. How did the room look?

> Uncle Harry delivered nine presents. He put twice as many under the tree as on the fireplace mantel. How did the room look?

First and second graders alike had grown in their ability to explain their solutions and to appreciate the strategies shared by others. Though we didn't push our first graders to write yet, many were able to move beyond simple addition and subtraction as they created picture problems for their classmates to solve. In fact, as some began crafting their problems, they wrote "?", "1/2", or "twice as many" on their closet doors before they did anything else. It was clear that they had definite problems in mind. Even though time ran out for us before the holiday break, the children were quite interested in continuing to solve one another's Presents problems in January.

Getting Started

ADDITION, SUBTRACTION, MULTIPLICATION & DIVISION

You will need...
- overheads of fireplace and door storyboards, Blacklines B61-B62
- overhead Christmas presents, 12, Blackline B1
- overhead Christmas parcels, 10, Blackline B80
- fireplace and door storyboards, 1 copy of each per student, Blacklines B61-B62
- Christmas presents, 12 per student, pp. 185-186
- parcels, 10 per student, Blackline B80

Begin the new theme by posing the Presents problems below. Ask children to work with their own storyboards and tiny presents to set up and solve the problems, but don't insist on the use of these manipulatives by all students if some are able to work mentally at times. (This is more likely to occur among second graders than first.) As your students solve the problems, encourage them to share their different strategies with others. It will take two class session, possibly longer, to get through this set. Second grade teachers may want to pass up the problems in the first three sections and move straight to Missing Addends/Missing Subtrahends (see page 82).

Note: You'll notice that some of these problems involve a fireplace mantel while others require a closet door. Because we were unable to fit a tree, mantel, and door on one sheet, we gave each student two storyboards, one with tree and mantel (the Fireplace board) and the other with tree and door (the Door board). Although this caused a slight confusion, we noticed that some of the children switched boards when necessary, while others were perfectly happy to pretend that the door was a fireplace mantel or vice versa. Either way was fine with us.

How Many Altogether?

● It was just past midnight when the small child awoke to the tinging of bells. Had Santa been there? The boy saw four presents under the tree and five on the fireplace mantel. How many presents were there altogether? *(Fireplace board)*

● It was early Christmas morning. The children raced down the stairs. They couldn't believe their eyes. There were nine presents under the tree and six on the fireplace mantel. How many altogether? *(Fireplace board)*

Adding Three or More Numbers

● What a wonderful time of year! Grandpa and Grandma arrived with a bagful of presents. Grandpa put six under the tree while Grandma placed four on the fireplace mantel. Later that evening, Aunt Nancy left three more under the tree. How many in all? *(Fireplace board)*

How Many Are Left?

● Santa's elf tiptoed into the room to deliver nine presents. He set four by the door and the rest under the tree. One, two, three, four, five, six, seven, eight, nine. Suddenly, the Grinch flung open the door and whisked away four of the gifts. How many were left? *(Door board)*

● There were eight gifts in the living room—six under the tree and two in front of the closet. The lady from the church stopped by to pick up the two gifts by the closet. How many were left? *(Door board)*

● The Grinch set three of the family's ten presents in front of the closet door. He was up to no good, and planned to take them to his sleigh. How did the room look? How many gifts would be left after his mischievous visit? *(Door board)*

....

Missing Addend / Missing Subtrahend

● The small boy peeked out from behind the tree. His sister had told him there were eleven gifts altogether, but he could only see six under the tree because the rest were hidden in the closet. How many were in the closet? *(Door board)*

....

Comparing Or Finding The Difference

● There were six presents on the fireplace mantel and four presents under the tree. How many fewer were under the tree? *(Fireplace board)*

Ginny: I can't do that kind. That's too hard.

Johnny: I got it! It's ten.

Teacher: If I had asked how many presents altogether, it would be ten. Listen one more time to the question. How many *fewer* were under the tree?

Kristen: Is that like "not so many"?

Teacher: That's one way to say it.

Kristen: How many were on the fireplace?

Teacher: There were six on the fireplace...and four under the tree.

Cory: I see how to do it. (Cory runs to the chalkboard and draws.)

Teacher: That sure worked for you. Did anyone have a different way to solve it?

Melissa: I took the ones out from under the tree—four of them and lined them up right over the presents on the fireplace. See, they each touch. I had two left over that didn't have any to touch. Is that what you mean—not so many?

Teacher: "How many fewer" is a confusing term for many of you. I always have to stop and think about it too. What if I asked how many *less* are under the tree than on the fireplace. Does that make it easier to figure it out?

Ginny: I'm still not sure what you mean.

Kristen: It really looks like two more, Ginny. I just try to pretend there are two empty spaces after the four presents. See? These two don't have partners.

Teacher: You are doing a wonderful job of working with a very difficult problem and trying hard to explain your thinking to others.

Before you move on, explain to students that you're going to be giving them problems that involve parcels of ten presents and be sure they have access to ten "parcels" each, in addition to the miniature presents they've been using. Either of the two storyboards, the Fireplace or the Door, will work for the set of problems below.

....

Working With Tens and Ones

✪ Mom was in charge of the Children's Hospital party. People had been leaving off parcels all day, and by late morning she had three parcels with ten presents in each. How many presents did she have altogether?

✪ That afternoon, two more parcels, each with ten presents, arrived. Now how many presents did she have?

✪ When Mom told her family that she had already collected fifty presents for the party, her children brought out six more they had made. What was the total now?

✪ The workers from the bank sent over twenty-two more gifts to add to Mom's collection. How many presents now?

Mark: But we don't have twenty-two presents to add. I only have nine!

Beth: Wait! We could make twenty-two by using two parcels and two presents—right?

Teacher: What do you think, girls and boys? If we want to add twenty-two presents to the fifty-six we already have, will it work to add two parcels and two presents?

Children: We'll have to—we don't have enough presents by themselves.

83

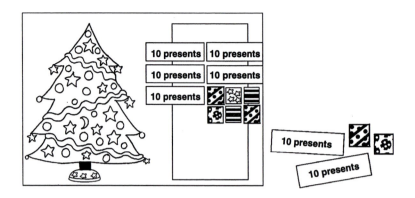

Teacher: If we do that, what's the total? What happens when we add twenty-two to fifty-six?

Children: It's seventy-eight! Wow, that's a lot of presents!

Teacher: Could someone explain how they arrived at the total?

Luce-Maria: I just looked at the parcels first. See, I have ten, twenty, thirty, forty, fifty, sixty, seventy, and then eight more—that's seventy-eight.

Timmy: I know that fifty plus twenty is seventy, and six plus two is eight—it's seventy-eight.

....

Working With Tens and Ones ✪ (continued)

✪ The Hospital Christmas party was only two days away, so Mom decided it was time to start delivering some of the seventy-eight presents she'd collected. One of her children offered to take eight of them to the hospital on his bicycle. How many presents were left then?

✪ One of the hospital workers arrived in a small car to take the remaining seventy presents, but could only carry forty of them. How many were still left at Mom's house?

....

Partitioning

● The small child was too excited to sleep. She sneaked down the stairs and saw seven presents. Some were under the tree and some were on the mantel. Can you show how the presents might have looked in that room? *(Fireplace board)*

Jacob: You mean there were seven in each place?

Teacher: No, there were seven presents altogether, but some of them were under the tree and some of them were on the fireplace mantel.

Ben: I don't get it.

84

Shajuanna: Just take seven presents—right? Now put some of them under the tree and some of them up on the mantel.

David: Can I put five under the tree and two on the mantel?

Shajuanna: Sure!

Teacher: Are there any other possibilities?

Children: I put four under the tree and three on the mantel. Not me—I have six under my tree and just one on the mantel. I just turned that around—I have one under the tree and six on the mantel.

Teacher: So there are all kinds of ways to arrange seven presents using those two locations on your board?

Children: Right!

Teacher: Now let's try a slightly different challenge.

....

Partitioning (continued)

● Santa's elf delivered five presents. She tucked one more present under the tree than on the fireplace mantel. How many were in each place? *(Fireplace board)*

Sanda: That's easy. There were five presents on the mantel and six under the tree—six is one more than five.

Teacher: That's true, but the elf delivered *only five* presents.

Josh: But you said there was one more under the tree than on the mantel.

Teacher: Is there any way to arrange five presents in such a way that there are some under the tree and some on the mantel?

Anna: We could put four under the tree and one on the mantel.

Teacher: That's a good suggestion. If we do that, how many more are under the tree than on the mantel?

Children: Four? No, three. Yeah, three, because both the tree and the mantel have one, but the tree has three more.

Teacher: Is there any way to arrange these five presents so that there's only one more under the tree than on the mantel? Maybe you could try moving the presents around on your board a bit.

The problem here is to keep the total in mind—five—while manipulating the parts so that x differs from y by one $(x + y = 5$ and $y = x + 1)$. Many of our second graders enjoyed this challenge in December, but needed quite a bit of help at first. We also tried it with our first graders and found that a few were quite tickled as they tried to figure it out. Others were totally lost. Be sure to offer several problems of this sort, and don't despair if a fair number of your students don't seem to understand right away. You can come back with this format later in the school year.

Partitioning (continued)

✪ There were ten presents in the living room, two more under the tree than in front of the closet door. How did the room look? The gifts by the closet were to be taken to the hospital Christmas party. How many would be left? *(Door board)*

✪ Uncle Harry delivered nine presents. He put twice as many under the tree as on the fireplace mantel. How did the room look? *(Fireplace board)*

Twice As Many / Multiplication

● Two small children were peeking from behind the tree. Their mom said there were four presents for each of them hidden in the closet. How many were in the closet? *(Door board)*

● There were three presents under the tree and twice as many in the closet. How many were in the closet? How many were there in all? *(Door board)*

Half As Many / Division

● Santa's elf placed six gifts under the tree and half that many in the closet. How many gifts were in the closet? How many gifts altogether? *(Door board)*

If "half as many" is still difficult for some of your students, encourage their classmates to offer explanations. One of our favorites was volunteered by a first grader who held up ten fingers and had his best friend "chop" between them. When he saw that some of the children still didn't understand, he had them each hold up four fingers and "cut them down the middle" with the "chopper hand". For weeks after, many children used Brandon's "chopper method" to solve similar problems.

● Santa's elf left ten presents in the room. Half were under the tree and half were in front of the fireplace. How did the room look? *(Fireplace board)*

✪ The two children know that their mom and dad have hidden sixteen gifts in the closet for them to share equally. How many gifts will each child receive? *(Door board)*

Creating Story Problems

In December, we still present models of story problems in both pictures and words, which children examine and then solve. After working with our problem models, children go on to create their own picture or picture/word story problems. Some copy or modify our ideas only slightly, while others are able to invent their own pictorial, written, or mathematical twists. Although nearly all second graders can be expected to write stories to accompany their picture problems at this point, most first graders will be more comfortable posing story problems in picture form only.

EXAMINING SOME POSSIBILITIES

You will need...

- Christmas Presents problem models, Blacklines B63-B79
- Fireplace and Door storyboard blacklines, 1 copy per student, Blacklines B61-B62
- Christmas presents, 12 per student, pp. 185-186
- parcels, 10 per student, Blackline B80

Note: If you are a second grade teacher, consider omitting some of the easier problem models and featuring those marked with a star. Our models aren't as challenging as some of the examples in the Getting Started section because they're meant to help children write their own story problems. We find that most primary students aren't able to pose problems at quite the level they can solve them. Your more capable second graders may find their own ways to "soup up" even some of the easier problem models, however. If you are a first grade teacher, you'll probably want to limit your choice of problem models to five or six. Don't shy away from the multiplication and division models, though. This was the month that many of our first graders really began to understand the concepts of "twice as many" and "half as many" well enough to use them in their own problems.

Begin by asking children to examine the picture portion of one of your problem models. Can they figure out what the problem is by looking at the picture alone? Show them the written story problem on the flap. Does the story help to clarify the problem to be solved?

Teacher: I've put together a new story problem for you to solve today. Although the words for this story problem are tucked up behind the picture on a flap, I'm curious to know if you can figure out what the problem is simply by looking at the picture.

Children: There are four kids peeking at that bag. It says something on the bag. They think there are presents inside. They think all of the presents are for them. Wait! I can read it. It says on the bag that they get three each.

Teacher: So what do you think the picture is asking you to figure out?

Children: Is it how many presents each kid would get? No, it's how many are in the bag altogether. It's three for each person. Does that bag lift up? Can we see what's under the bag? I've got it, I think. Three and three are six. Six and six make twelve. I think it's twelve. I got that too. I counted on my fingers.

Teacher: Let's fold down the flap at the bottom of the page and read the story that goes along with the picture to see if there's a match between your thinking and the written part of the problem.

Children: We did it! We got the problem from looking at the picture! It's neat that you can tell a story problem with only a picture. Yeah! You don't have to write so much. But I like writing a story to go along with my picture.

Have students examine each of your problem models, discussing, reading, and solving the problems as they go. We find that children often solve our picture/word problems in the process of examining them, but they can certainly use their counters and boards to arrive at solutions if necessary. Once all your problem models have been examined, display them in a prominent area at eye level so students can think about which they might like to copy or modify when they create their own story problems.

CHRISTMAS PRESENTS PROBLEM MODELS

To make copies of these problem models for use in your own classroom, see Blacklines B63-B79.

**Problem
Model 1**

Her brother told her there were nine gifts in the living room but she could only see four under the tree. Perhaps the rest were hidden in the closet. How many might be in the closet?

**Problem
Model 2**

It was Christmas Eve. Four gifts were already under the tree. The child's aunt and uncle had arrived with three more gifts. How many gifts in all?

CHRISTMAS PRESENTS PROBLEM MODELS (CONT.)

Problem Model 3

Santa's boots could be seen as he was leaving the house. He had placed three gifts on the fireplace mantel and eight under the tree. How many more were under the tree than on the mantel?

Problem Model 4

There were six gifts under the tree and half as many in the closet. How many were in the closet? How many gifts altogether?

CHRISTMAS PRESENTS PROBLEM MODELS (CONT.)

Problem Model 5

Grandpa told the curious child there were twice as many gifts in the closet as under the tree. The girl counted six under the tree. How many were in the closet? How many altogether?

Problem Model 6

Santa had left a secret bag by the tree. On the side, it said "3 for each". The four children were trying to figure out how many gifts were in the bag altogether.

CHRISTMAS PRESENTS PROBLEM MODELS (CONT.)

Problem Model 7

Santa had barely started up the chimney when three girls peeked out from behind the tree. There were twelve presents with the girls' names on them. How many did each girl get to open?

Problem Model 8

○ Mom was collecting gifts for the children's hospital party and putting them in parcels of ten. So far she had collected 36 gifts and stored them in the closet. How did her closet look?

CHRISTMAS PRESENTS PROBLEM MODELS (CONT.)

✪
**Problem
Model 9**

> ✪ Dad had been shopping for gifts for all of the children who would be coming to his company's family Christmas party. He wanted to give two gifts to each of the 16 youngsters. How many gifts did he need to buy? If he stored them in parcels of ten, how did his closet look?

Crafting Story Problems

You will need...

- 9" x 12" black construction paper, 1 sheet per student, *or* Door or Fireplace storyboard blacklines, 1 copy per student (see Note below)

- 3 x 5 pieces of brown construction paper for closet doors, 1 per student

- assorted sizes and colors of construction paper for story characters and other details

- "mini curls" fake hair, available at many craft and fabric stores (optional but quite charming)

- white construction paper in various sizes to make "talking bubbles" for question marks, words, and numbers that signal the problems to be solved

- Christmas presents, 10 to 12 for each student; pp. 185-186

- precut Christmas trees and fireplaces*

- white glue, scissors, crayons

- parcels to share, 5 per student, Blackline B80

  additional materials for second graders:

- student writing paper and pencils

- 4½" x 12" black construction paper for story flaps, 1 per student*

Note: Before you gather the materials to have your children create their own story problems, think about whether you want them to start from scratch using black construction paper backgrounds or whether you want them to start with blackline copies of the Door or Fireplace storyboard. Starting with blackline copies of the storyboards is somewhat easier in that children have only to color and add details, but starting from scratch produces more charming results. Kristen, whose work is shown above, started with black construction paper. She used a precut closet door and presents, decorated a precut tree to her own liking, and created her own characters. If students create their story problems from scratch, you'll need the items above marked with an asterisk (*), in addition to the other materials listed.

When all the problem models have been examined and solved, display them where children can easily refer to each kind as they create their own problems for others to solve. Even though this may be the third time your students have approached this task, some will still copy your models almost exactly, changing only the numbers.

Other students, particularly second graders, may modify your ideas or insert their own unique twists, especially if you encourage them to create problems that will interest and challenge their classmates. Don't be discouraged if you wind up with seventeen missing-addend stories, five "twice as many", and a few examples of subtraction or division. We found again and again that the problems our students posed reflected their actual developmental levels, as opposed to the higher levels of problem solving they demonstrated under our guidance in group settings.

Explain that you want each child to prepare a Presents story problem to pose to the rest of the class. It is important that the picture portion pose the problem as clearly as possible and, for second graders, that the written portion support the picture with all needed details. You may also want to limit the number of presents your students can use in their own problems. We held our first graders to twenty-five or fewer; our second graders were allowed to use up to fifty.

Most second graders will want to begin with the picture part of their problems and may need another day before they're able to finish the written part. When children's story problems are complete, encourage them to check with classmates to see if their work makes sense. Can other children understand what needs to be solved? Have they posed problems that can be solved by peers? Finally, have youngsters meet with you for final conferencing or editing as needed. Some first graders may need to explain their thinking to you and may even want to dictate a written portion. Second graders may need to refine a question or clarify their story in some way.

Second grade teachers will need to type or print each child's problems on a 3½" x 11" strip of white paper, using standard spelling and punctuation. Since we both have Macintosh computers, we like to use a bold 36 point font with a sideways page set-up. That way we can type the whole batch of story problems at once, print them out, and cut them apart. Most computers have a 24 point font, if not a 36. If you don't have access to a computer, you can print children's problems with wide-tip black felt marker. The point is to wind up with good quality print large enough to be read at a distance.

The next day, have your second graders tape the typed story flaps to their picture problems along the bottom. If they have worked from scratch on construction paper instead of copies of the storyboard, they'll need to glue their typed or printed strips to the pieces of construction paper precut for this activity and then tape the flaps along the bottom of their pictures.

Also, have each child glue the draft copy of his or her writing to the back of his or her picture—incorporating the rough draft into a finished product validates children's hard work and can be a nice source of information about students' growing capabilities in the areas of writing and spelling.

Santa put 22 presents under the tree and 16 on the mantel. How many more under the tree?

by Johnny

Solving Student Problems

You will need...

- student problems, select 5 to 6
- Fireplace and Door storyboard blacklines, 1 copy per student, Blacklines B61-B62
- Christmas presents, 12 per student, pp. 185-186
- 8½" x 14" paper, 1 sheet per student
- pencils with erasers
- chalkboards to serve as hard writing surfaces if you're able to gather your children into a group meeting area on the rug
- parcels, 5 per student, Blackline B80

Once children have completed their own story problems, it's sharing time. This is the phase that develops a child's sense of audience—their awareness that they are, in fact, writing to interest and challenge their classmates. For this reason, we try to feature every story, if not during a whole-group sharing session, then in a class book, wall display, or as part of a homework assignment.

We usually select five to six particularly interesting, unique, or challenging student problems for initial presentation to the group, however. As in previous sessions, children are seated on the rug with paper, pencils, and easy access to problem-solving materials. This late in the year, we encourage first and second graders alike to try to set down their strategies and solutions on paper before we do much discussion. As we move through each problem, some children work mentally and record their thinking in numbers and/or words. It's very common for these students to illustrate their thinking in pictures as well. Some youngsters use sketches or diagrams to solve problems, sometimes labeling their work with words or giving some sort of brief written explanation. Still others use manipulatives (even their fingers) and recreate their work in drawn or written form on the paper.

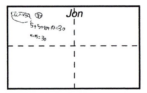

Before you pose the first student problem, have each child fold a piece of 8½" x 14" paper into four sections and write his or her name at the top. After children have set up their papers, present one problem at a time (or have the student author present it), allow time for questions or clarification, and have students spend some time working on their own at the rug. Expect some amount of interchange, especially among first graders, and plenty of looking around and imitation on the part of those who don't quite "get it". After a few minutes, ask those who are willing to share their solutions and explain their strategies.

Second Grade Teacher: What do you notice about the picture portion of Laura's problem?

Children: There are a lot of presents. She used parcels. There are a lot. One of the kids has a question mark over her head. That's for how many in all.

Teacher: Laura, would you like to read the story flap on your problem so we're sure of what you want us to do?

Laura: Sure!

Under the tree there were 5 presents. Then Mom went down the stairs. She put 15 under the tree. Then Dad came down the stairs and he put 10 presents under the tree. How many altogether?

Children: It *is* how many in all! All we have to do is add the numbers!

After working for a minute or two, most of the children agreed that the total was thirty. Some worked with parcels and presents on their boards, while others counted what they could see in Laura's picture. Still others were able to add the three numbers mentally, but all faced the challenge of recording their thinking on paper.

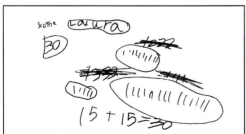

Scottie used tally marks to arrive at a solution, drawing out five, then ten, then fifteen. He counted them and recorded 15 + 15 = 30, apparently realizing that the group of five and the group of ten could be combined to make a group of fifteen.

Johnny's initial response was to break the numbers into chunks that he could total very quickly.

Since Laura already knew the answer to her own problem, she expressed it in several different number sentences, using multiplication as well as division.

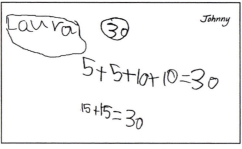

Johnny's response

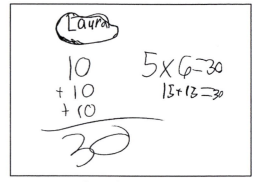

Laura's response

The thing that was most intriguing to us about the children's responses to Laura's problem was that so many of them expressed their thinking in number sentences. Apparently, addition had become familiar enough, and these particular numbers easy enough to add, that numbers were a convenient shorthand. This was a signal to us that straightforward addition had ceased, perhaps, to pose a problem to some of our second graders.

Plan to go through five to six student problems in the first sharing session. You'll probably want to save samples of children's written responses to classmates' story problems, both to get a sense of the various strategies students are using and also to characterize individuals' strategies or specific math skills.

While it's important to acknowledge each child's story problem, it's difficult to get through more than half the class, even in two or three sharing sessions. Here are some suggestions for honoring story problems not featured in class sharing sessions:

• Post the entire collection on one of your classroom walls after the first few have been shared with the class. Admire and read a few daily with your class.

• Post the collection in a display area outside the classroom. We have frequently seen children from other classrooms stop and try to figure out problems written by their friends.

• Work the more challenging problems together during one of two sharing sessions and save the rest to serve as "sponge activities": many of the problems our students pose can be solved mentally and make wonderful two- or three-minute fillers before lunch or recess.

• Bind the story problems into mini-books to be enjoyed during math or reading time.

• Send home collections of student problems for homework. In first grade, we make reduced copies of four student problems per week. We mount them two per sheet and make sure that we "publish" at least one problem from each student over the course of the year. In second grade, we type the entire collection and ask our students to select ten to twelve to work and return.

---

name _____

Math Homework - Week of December 13 - 17

Please do at least ten of the Presents story problems in this collection. (You're welcome to do more, of course.) These are the problems your friends in class wrote last week, and some of them are pretty hard. Be sure to show your thinking in words, numbers, or diagrams under each problem you decide to do; if you only give the answers, I won't know how you figured things out. If you want to borrow some parcels and presents from the Presents story box, or some base ten blocks for a few days, please let me know.

It was the first night of Hannukah. There were five kids, and 16 presents. How many will the kids each get, if the mom gets one?

Ashley L.

Four kids slept downstairs looking for Santa. When Santa came they were asleep. But he left 8 presents for each kid. How many presents altogether?

Ella

There were 31 presents. Santa left one more in the fireplace. There were 2 kids. How many presents did they each get?

Alex

Jill and Billy went downstairs. Their brother had said that there were 26 presents for them. But when they got there, they only saw 9 under the tree. How many were in the closet?

Laura V.

Santa brought 59 presents, but the children forgot to close the window and 22 presents got blown into the fire. How many presents were left?

Mason

Theme 3B

Presents for Special Occasions

F or teachers who don't choose to implement Christmas-related activities in their classrooms but like the idea of presents, we've included a variation on the theme—Presents for Special Occasions. In this section, you'll find problems geared to the giving and receiving of presents for birthdays, anniversaries, and other non-holiday related occasions. Although the problems and problem models are different, the routines for teaching the lessons are nearly identical to Christmas Presents and we ask you to refer to pages 79–99 in addition to the notes below for instructions and insights. To make alternate storyboards, counters, and problem models, please see Preparation of Materials.

Getting Started

ADDITION, SUBTRACTION, MULTIPLICATION & DIVISION

You will need...

- overheads of Fireplace and Door storyboards for Special Occasions, Blacklines B81-B82
- overhead presents for Special Occasions, 12, Blackline B1
- overhead parcels, 10, Blackline B80
- Fireplace and Door storyboards for Special Occasions, 1 copy per student, Blacklines B81-B82
- presents for Special Occasions, 12 per student, pp. 185-186
- parcels, 10 per student, Blackline B80

Begin this theme by posing the problems below and asking children to work with their storyboards and miniature presents. As your students solve the problems, encourage them to share the different strategies they're using. It will probably take two class sessions or more to cover this set of problems. Second grade teachers may want to emphasize the starred problems. For additional teaching tips and insights, please read Christmas Presents, Getting Started, pages 80-87.

....

How Many Altogether?

● The small child awoke to the sweet smell of a birthday cake baking. He ran into the family room and saw four presents on the table and five on the fireplace mantel. How many presents were there altogether? *(Fireplace board)*

● What a great party it would be! It was Grandpa and Grandma's twenty-fifth anniversary. The whole family was coming! There were six presents on the table and six on the fireplace mantel. How many presents in all? *(Fireplace board)*

....

Adding Three or More Numbers

✪ Many of the neighborhood families decided to have a block party for the fourth of July. They thought it would be fun to wrap up a small gift for each of the children. One family brought five giant balloons, another family donated eight poppers, and the everyone else chipped in some money to buy six small flags. How many gifts were they able to wrap up? *(Either board)*

101

How Many Are Left?

● Everyone was having lots of fun at the block party. The man who was dressed like Uncle Sam began giving out small gifts to the youngest children. He began with a big box that held ten gifts and gave seven of them away. How many were left? *(Either board)*

Missing Addend / Missing Subtrahend

● There were nine gifts altogether. Six were on the table and the rest were on the fireplace mantel. How many were on the mantel? *(Fireplace board)*

● There were eleven presents in the room, seven on the table, the rest in the closet. How many were in the closet? *(Door board)*

Comparing or Finding The Difference

● The neighborhood kids decided to have a Back to School party. Their parents wrapped up pencils, notebook paper, pens, and erasers as small gifts for the children. They put six of the wrapped gifts on the table and four on the fireplace mantel. How many more gifts were on the table than on the fireplace mantel? *(Fireplace board)*

✪ Everyone was getting ready for a family reunion. Grandma had decided to wrap up little trinkets for each of the children who would be attending. Four of the gifts were on the table and twice as many were on the fireplace mantel. How many more were on the fireplace mantel? How many gifts had Grandma wrapped altogether? *(Fireplace board)*

Twice As Many

● There were five gifts on the table and twice as many hidden in the closet. How many gifts were in the closet? How many presents altogether? *(Door board)*

Half As Many

● Mom and her friends at work were planning a surprise party for their boss. The truck drivers brought twelve gifts. The warehouse workers brought half as many gifts. How many gifts did the warehouse workers bring? How many gifts did the boss get in all? *(Either board)*

Division: Sharing / Grouping

● The boss was so tickled that his employees had been working so hard that he brought in sixteen gifts for them to share. There were eight workers. If each worker got the same number of gifts, how many gifts did each one receive? *(Either board)*

Working In Tens & Ones

✪ Everyone in town was getting ready for a big celebration at the children's hospital. Dad was in charge. People were dropping off parcels of presents all day. By late morning, Dad had three parcels each with ten gifts. How many presents in all? *(Either board)*

✪ That afternoon, two more parcels of ten gifts arrived. Now how many gifts in all? *(Either board)*

✪ Some of Dad's friends brought seven gifts by. Now how many altogether? *(Either board)*

✪ The nurses came by to start delivering gifts. They needed twenty-two for the first ward. How many gifts were left? *(Either board)*

✪ They came back for twenty-five more. Now how many are left? *(Either board)*

Partitioning

● The small child was too excited to sleep. She sneaked down the stairs for a peek at her birthday presents. She saw seven altogether. Some were on the table, some on the fireplace mantel. One more was on the table than on the fireplace mantel. How many were in each place? *(Fireplace board)*

✪ There were ten presents in the living room, two more on the fireplace mantel than on the table. How did the room look? The gifts on the table were to be taken to the office party. How many would be left? *(Fireplace board)*

✪ There were twelve gifts in the room, four less on the fireplace mantel than on the table. How many were in each place? *(Fireplace board)*

Creating Story Problems

Once children have had an opportunity to work through a substantial number of the problems above, present models of story problems in picture and word form for students to examine and solve. After working with your problem models, have children create their own problems.

EXAMINING SOME POSSIBILITIES

You will need...

• Special Occasions problem models, 1 to 9, Blacklines B83-B98

• Fireplace and Door storyboards for Special Occasions, 1 copy per student, Blacklines B81-B82

• presents for Special Occasions, 12 per student, pp. 185-186

Below, you'll find illustrations showing the problem models for Special Occasions. To find out how to use these models to help children think about creating their own story problems, please refer to Christmas Presents, Examining Some Possibilities, pages 87-93.

SPECIAL OCCASIONS PROBLEM MODELS

To make copies of these problem models for use in your own classroom, see Blacklines B83-B98.

Problem Model 1

His brother told him there were nine gifts but he could only see four on the table. Perhaps the rest were hidden in the closet. How many might be in the closet?

SPECIAL OCCASIONS PROBLEM MODELS (CONT.)

Problem Model 2

The girl is six years old today. Her aunt and uncle have just set three more gifts on the table. Four gifts were already on the fireplace mantel. How many gifts will the child have in all?

Problem Model 3

It was nearly time for Grandpa and Grandma's anniversary. Everyone had been bringing gifts. There were four gifts on the fireplace mantel and six on the table. How many more were on the table than on the mantel?

SPECIAL OCCASIONS PROBLEM MODELS (CONT.)

Problem Model 4

There were six gifts on the table and half as many in the closet. How many were in the closet? How many gifts in all?

Problem Model 5

Grandpa told the curious child there were twice as many gifts in the closet as on the table. The girl counted seven on the table. How many were in the closet? How many altogether?

SPECIAL OCCASIONS PROBLEM MODELS (CONT.)

Problem Model 6

The triplets are seven years old today. There is a sign on the closet door that says, "four presents each". How many gifts are in the closet altogether?

Problem Model 7

All the relatives had gone to the living room. The two cousins tiptoed into the room. There were twelve presents for them to share. How many will each cousin get?

SPECIAL OCCASIONS PROBLEM MODELS (CONT.)

✪
**Problem
Model 8**

✪ Mom will be shopping for gifts for the sixteen
children who will attend the church potluck party. She
wants to give two gifts to each of the youngsters.
How many gifts does she need to buy? If she stores
them in parcels of ten, how will her closet look?

**Problem
Model 9**

The pediatric nurses are collecting gifts for the
children's hospital party and storing them in a big
closet in parcels of ten. So far, they have collected 42
gifts. How does the closet look?

Crafting Story Problems

You will need...

- 9" x 12" pastel construction paper, 1 sheet per student, *or* Door or Fireplace storyboards for Special Occasions, 1 copy per student, Blackline B81 or B82, (see Note below)

- 3" x 5" pieces of brown construction paper for closet doors, 1 per student

- assorted sizes and colors of construction paper for story characters and other details

- "mini curls" fake hair, available at many craft and fabric stores (optional but quite charming)

- Special Occasions presents, 10 to 12 for each student, pp. 185-186

- white construction paper in various sizes to make "talking bubbles" for question marks, words, and numbers that signal the problems to be solved

- precut tables and fireplaces*

- white glue, scissors, crayons

- parcels, 5 per student, Blackline B80

  additional materials for second graders:

- student writing paper and pencils

- 4½" x 12" pastel construction paper for story flaps, 1 per student*

*Note: Before you gather the materials to have your children create their own story problems, think about whether you want them to start from scratch, using pastel construction paper backgrounds, or whether you want them to start with blackline copies of the Special Occasion storyboards. Starting with blackline copies of the storyboards is somewhat easier, in that children have only to color in tables and fireplaces, and add their own characters and precut presents, but starting from scratch often produces more charming results. If you decide to have student create their story problems from scratch, you'll need the items above marked with an asterisk (*), **in addition to** the other materials listed.*

Please refer to Christmas Presents, Crafting Story Problems, pages 93-95, for information on helping children create their own picture/word story problems with the materials listed above.

Solving Student Problems

You will need...

- student problems, select 5 or 6
- Fireplace and Door storyboards for Special Occasions, Blacklines B81-B82
- Special Occasion presents, 12 per student, pp. 185-186
- 8$\frac{1}{2}$" x 14" paper, 1 sheet per student
- pencils with erasers, 1 per student
- chalkboards to serve as hard writing surfaces if you're able to gather your children into a group meeting area on the rug
- parcels, 5 per student, Blackline B80

For advice about helping children solve one another's story problems, please see Christmas Presents, Solving Student Problems, pages 96-99.

The
Teddy Bear
Store

Theme 4

The Teddy Bear Store

T he Teddy Bear Store is divided into three parts: Teddy Bear Deliveries, Buying and Selling Teddy Bears, and Graphing Teddy Bear Sales. The Problems in Part I revisit every whole number operation already introduced, with a new twist—thinking in terms of fives and ones. A straightforward addition problem involves two steps now, as children figure out how many bears there are in four crates before they compute the store's new total:

> The bear store owner has three white bears on the shelf. She wants the
> truck to deliver four crates of white bears. If each crate holds five bears,
> how many white bears will she have in all?

We recommend that you devote a week or more to Part I. Pose the suggested problems in oral and written form, then have your students develop their own story problems.

Return to the Teddy Bear Store a month later to work on Part II, in which children use pretend bills (ones,

111

fives, and tens) to pay for white bears and brown bears priced at four and five dollars, respectively. The first few problems in this section are relatively direct. Students are asked to compute totals for purchases of three brown bears; four white bears; two browns and three whites; and so on. The next few problems involve some higher-level thinking as children are challenged to figure out what can be purchased with given sums of money:

> Cory came into the bear store with $17.00 to spend. He was very happy when he found out the bears were on sale for four and five dollars apiece. What was he able to buy?

Because the problem doesn't dictate whether or not Cory left with any change in his pocket, there are many possible solutions. It's conceivable that Cory only bought one brown bear, and had twelve dollars left to spend elsewhere. Then again, he may have decided to spend the entire sum at the bear shop. Many primary children find these problems most intriguing, but do not solve them quickly or easily.

Again, we suggest that you devote another week, perhaps a little longer, to the problems in Part II. Pose suggested story problems orally and in written form, and then have children create their own. The graphing problems in Part III take no more than a day or two and offer closure on the theme of buying and selling teddy bears.

HOW IT WORKED FOR US

After winter break, our students were quite eager to explore another story problem theme. By then, nearly all of them had developed a degree of confidence with the addition and subtraction formats we'd introduced so far. Many were eager to do more work with multiplication and division. The problems we posed included all of the addition, subtraction, multiplication, and division formats previously addressed but, after a few Getting Started sessions, it was apparent we could increase the challenges. We turned some of the "how many more" problems into partitioning situations.

> There were seven bears on the shelves, one more on the top shelf than on the second shelf. How many were on each shelf?

Because the theme revolved around a store, we could pose problems involving money and design simple sales graphs. It also made sense to include problems about shipping bears in crates of five. We marched forward knowing there would be disequilibrium (even a touch of chaos) as well as joy. We also decided it was time to ask first graders to try writing their own problems rather than relying on pictures alone. Many found it very challenging but most persevered.

Our second graders began to exchange problems with children from other classes, which gave them even more reason to communicate their problem-solving strategies clearly via drawings, numbers, or words. We had intended to finish this theme by the end of January in our own classrooms, but we found ourselves coming back to it well into March because of the wonderful new challenges The Teddy Bear Store provided.

I: Teddy Bear Deliveries

Getting Started

ADDITION, SUBTRACTION, MULTIPLICATION & DIVISION

You will need...
- overhead of The Teddy Bear Store storyboard, Blackline B99
- overhead teddy bears, 16, Blackline B1
- overhead bear crates, 10 of each color, Blackline B114
- The Teddy Bear Store storyboard, 1 copy per student, Blackline B99
- teddy bears, 8 of each color per student, p. 185
- bear crates, 10 of each color per student, Blackline B114

Begin the new theme by posing the problems below and asking children to work with their storyboards, teddy bear counters, and crates. As your students solve the problems, encourage them to share the different strategies they're trying. It will probably take two or three class sessions to cover this set of problems. Second grade teachers may want to leave out some of the easier examples and feature those marked with a star.

....

How Many Altogether?

● The teddy bear store had five brown bears on the top shelf and four white bears on the second shelf. How many bears did they have in stock?

✪ The Bear Shop had twenty-six brown bears and nineteen white bears. How many in all?

Children: How many brown bears? Twenty-six? That's too many! We don't have twenty-six brown bears!

Teacher: That's true. You don't. What can you do to solve the problem?

Ryan: I can solve it in my head, I think.

JoDell: Even if we put our bears together we wouldn't have enough. But what if we used the crates?

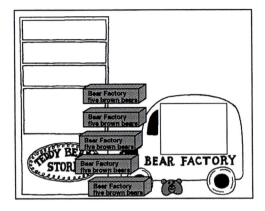

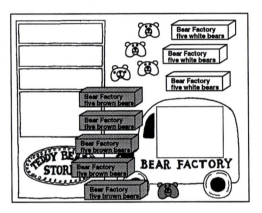

Children: Yes, the crates! Let's see...five, ten, fifteen, twenty, twenty-five, and one more brown bear. It's like the store just got a delivery and hasn't unpacked the crates yet.

Teacher: So you figure you can show the brown bears by using five crates and one more bear?

Children: Yes, and we need...five, ten, fifteen, twenty...no, five, ten, fifteen, sixteen, seventeen, eighteen, nineteen—three crates of white and four white bean bears. Now, what do we have to do with all these bears?

Brenton: We have to add them up. I already know how many there are.

Children: Don't tell ! I can just count my crates by fives to figure it out. Me, too—five, ten, fifteen, twenty, twenty-five, thirty, thirty-five, forty, forty-one, forty-two, forty-three, forty-four, forty-five. There are eight crates and five bean bears. We could trade them in for another five, except some are white and some are brown.

Teacher: So the total is forty-five?

Timmy: I figured it out a different way. I knew as soon as you said twenty-six and nineteen. It's forty-five, because it's almost like twenty-six plus twenty. That would be forty-six, but it's one less because we only added nineteen.

Teacher: Okay! Did anyone have a different way of thinking about this problem?

Rachel: I just thought about twenty plus ten. That made thirty. Then I hooked on the nine for thirty-nine and counted on six more to get up to forty-five.

Teacher: You certainly found some interesting ways to think about this problem.

Adding Three or More Numbers

● The teddy bear store shelves held four brown bears and six white bears. The truck was delivering five more bears. How many bears would the store have in all?

How Many Are Left?

● Bear sales had been a little slow at the toy store. The bear factory said the storekeeper could return five of his eleven bears. After the truck picked up the five bears, how many did he have left?

✪ Bear sales had been a little slow at the toy store. The bear factory said the storekeeper could return nine of his sixteen bears. After the truck picked up the nine bears, how many did he have left?

Missing Addend / Missing Subtrahend

● The teddy bear store was running low on bears. They had only five on their shelves and needed the truck to deliver enough so they would have eleven bears altogether. How many will the truck need to bring?

✪ The teddy bear store was running low on bears. They had only seven on their shelves and needed the truck to deliver enough so they would have sixteen bears altogether. How many will the truck need to bring?

Comparing or Finding The Difference

● The top shelf held four white teddy bears, the second shelf held six brown bears. How many fewer bears were on the top shelf than on the second shelf? How many bears were on the shelves in all?

✪ The delivery truck had twenty-one bears stacked inside and the store had nine bears on its shelves. How many more were there in the truck than in the store?

Working With Tens, Fives & Ones

● The bear store was preparing for a big sale. They ordered five crates of bears. Each crate held five bears. How many bears would the store have in all when the crates were unpacked?

● The bear store owner has three white bears on the shelf. She wants the truck to deliver four crates of white bears. If each crate holds five bears, how many white bears will she have in all?

115

Twice As Many

● There were three brown bears on the shelf and twice as many arriving in the truck. How many were in the truck? How many bears will the store have in all?

✪ There were seven white bears on the shelf and twice as many arriving in the truck. How many were in the truck? How many bears will the store have in all?

Half As Many

● The teddy bear store had eight bears on the shelves. They ordered half as many more from the bear factory. How many will the truck bring? How many will they have altogether?

Division: Sharing/Grouping

● The teddy bear store had four bears in stock. The truck would be delivering twenty more. How many crates would the truck bring? What would their new total be?

● The bears were trying to trick the store owner, so they were hiding behind the shelves and only their ears were sticking out. When she walked in, she could see fourteen ears. How many bears were hiding?

✪ The store was preparing for a sale and they needed lots more bears. They ordered twenty-five brown bears and thirty white bears. How many crates of bears will the truck need to deliver?

Partitioning

● There were five bears on the shelves. Some were on the top shelf, some were on the second shelf. There was one more bear on the second shelf than on the top shelf. How many bears were on each shelf?

✪ There were eleven bears on the shelves. Some were brown and some were white. Three more were brown than white. How many bears of each color were on the shelves?

✪ The bear store owner ordered nine bears; she wanted twice as many browns as whites. How many did she order of each color?

Cory: That's hard. Did you say nine altogether?

Teacher: Yes, nine altogether. Twice as many are brown as white.

Missy: I've got it. It's nine whites and eighteen browns. Can I borrow somebody's brown bears so I'll have enough to show you?

Cory: But that isn't nine altogether.

Missy: But eighteen is nine two times.

Teacher: If we were asking for twice as many as nine, you'd be exactly right. But the store only ordered nine bears altogether.

Cory: I think this would work. I'll put out two brown bears and then one white bear. Then two more brown bears and one white bear. Now I'm up to six. I need two more brown bears and one white bear. I think it's six brown bears and three white bears.

Kristen: I tried putting out four and two at first but that just made six. So then I put out two more browns and one more white to make it nine. I ended up the same as Cory—six and three.

Teacher: Did anyone work on it in a different way?

Ryan: I just knew it was six and three. They add up to nine and six is twice as many as three.

Melissa: I put out some brown bears and some white bears till I got nine. Then I counted. It wasn't twice as much so I kept changing it and counting until it worked.

··

Mixed Operations

✪ The truck was loaded with six crates, each with five bears. After they delivered sixteen bears to one teddy bear store, how many did they have left?

Danny: Wait a minute. We only have six. You can't take away sixteen.

Derek: I think you can. It's six crates. The truck has six crates—not just six bears.

Children: That's it. Five bears are in each crate. Five, ten, fifteen,

117

twenty, twenty-five, thirty. Thirty bears! We should be able to take sixteen away. Look! You can take fifteen away by taking out three crates. Let's see...five, ten, fifteen!

Teacher: Great so far! How many more bears do you need to take off the truck?

Children: One more. But we only have crates. Oh, I think I know how. Could I give the store the crate with five and have them give me back four bears?

Lisa: But she didn't say whether the store has any bears.

Teacher: It is a possible solution if the store has some bears. You're doing some fine thinking. Can you think of another way to solve it?

Robby: We all have some bears. Couldn't we just trade one crate in and put out five of our bears?

Teacher: That sounds like another good idea.

Children: If we trade a crate and get five bears, we'll have to give the store one of them and leave four on the truck. That works. Now we've got four bears and two crates. That makes twenty-four. No, not twenty-four. Oops, I counted by tens. There are five in each crate. Two fives and four—fourteen.

Teacher: Great problem solving. Let's try another one like that.

....

Mixed Operations (continued)

✪ The truck had thirty-seven bears. After they delivered nineteen to the teddy bear store, how many did they have left?

Children: Oh, no. That's even harder. How many bears did the truck have?

Teacher: They had thirty-seven bears.

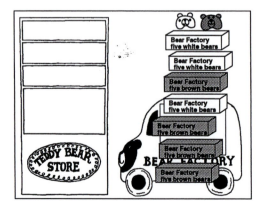

Children: One crate is five, two crates make ten, three crates...just count it by fives as you put them in. Five, ten, fifteen, twenty, twenty-five, thirty, thirty-five, forty. Oops! How many? Thirty-seven. You have to get two bean bears. Seven crates and two bean bears!

Teacher: Good job! Now you have to deliver nineteen bears to the bear store. What can you do?

Jacob: I want to give them four crates and have the store give me back one bear.

Children: She didn't say the store had any bears. And even if they did, they'd already be on the shelf. They might like them and not want to give one back.

Teacher: Let's assume they don't have any they'd want to trade, but that surely could have worked. What else could you try?

Janet: I think you have to give them three crates for the fifteen. But I don't know how to give them nineteen.

Jacob: Couldn't we trade a crate in again and get five of our bean bears?

Teacher: Try it and see what you can figure out.

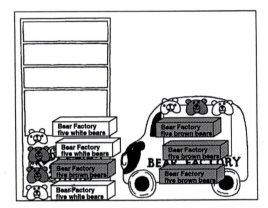

Kristen: I've got it! You trade it and get five, then put four of them with the three crates. Five, ten, fifteen, sixteen, seventeen, eighteen, nineteen. Now the truck only has three crates and three bears left—fifteen, sixteen, seventeen, eighteen.

Children: Show us that again—not so fast.

- -

Mixed Operations (continued)

✪ The truck was to deliver some crates of bears, five in each crate. There would be four crates of white bears and three crates of brown bears. How many white bears had the store ordered? How many brown bears? How many bears altogether?

✪ There are two white bears and four brown bears on the store shelves. The owner wants the truck to bring enough crates so that he'll have twelve white bears and nineteen brown bears. How many crates of each color will the truck need to bring? How many bears will the store have altogether?

119

Creating Story Problems

Once children have had an opportunity to work through a substantial number of the problems above, present models of story problems in picture and word form for students to examine and solve. After working with your models, have children create their own problems. You may want to ask your first graders to try writing the story portion of their problems this time.

EXAMINING SOME POSSIBILITIES

You will need...
- Teddy Bear Deliveries problem models, Blacklines B100-B107 and B118-B123
- The Teddy Bear Store storyboard, 1 copy per student, Blackline B99
- teddy bears, 8 of each color per student, p. 185
- bear crates, 10 of each color per student, Blackline B114

Note: If you are a second grade teacher, consider omitting some of the easier problem models for Part I and featuring those with stars. Our models aren't as challenging as some of the examples in the Getting Started section because they're meant to help children write their own story problems, and we find that most primary students aren't able to pose problems at quite the level they can solve them. Your more capable second graders may find their own ways to "soup up" even some of the easier problem models, however.

Begin by asking children to examine the picture portion of one of your problem models. Can they figure out what the problem is by looking at the picture alone? Show them the written story problem on the flap. Does the story help to clarify the problem to be solved?

Teacher: I've put together some new problem models for you to solve today. Although the written story problem is hidden, I'm eager to know if you can figure out what the problem is just by looking at the picture.

Children: There are nine bears on the shelf. Oh, wait a minute—there's a sign on the truck door. It says, "Twice as many". I bet we're supposed to figure out how many are in the truck. Yeah—twice as many. That's easy!

Teacher: Great detective work. Let's look at the written part of the problem on the flap below the picture to see if it provides any more information.

Bears had been selling so well that the store keeper put in a new order. She asked the bear factory to send twice the number of bears she already had on the shelves. How many did they send? How many did she have altogether?

Children: We did it. We figured it out with just the picture. The only part we didn't get was about adding all the bears together.

Teacher: You did that very well. You've had a lot of practice this year.

Have students examine each of your problem models, discussing, reading, and solving the problems as they go. We find that children often solve our picture/word problems mentally in the process of examining them, but they can certainly use the bears, crates, and boards as well. Once all your problem models have been examined, display them in a prominent area at eye level so students can think about which they might like to copy or modify when they create their own story problems.

TEDDY BEAR DELIVERIES PROBLEM MODELS

To make copies of these problem models for use in your own classroom, see Blacklines B100-B108, Blackline B113, and B118-B123.

Problem Model 1

The clerk at the bear store wants to have the same number of white bears as brown bears. How many more white bears will she need to have the factory deliver?

THE TEDDY BEAR DELIVERIES PROBLEM MODELS (CONT.)

Problem Model 2

The bear store owner wants to have eleven bears on display, but he has only six on his shelves. How many will the truck need to bring?

Problem Model 3

The brand new bear store is finally ready to open. They want to display four bears on each of their three shelves. How many bears will the factory need to bring?

THE TEDDY BEAR DELIVERIES PROBLEM MODELS (CONT.)

Problem Model 4

The teddy bears are playing tricks. Only their ears are peeking out from behind the shelf doors. How many bears will the storekeeper find when he peeks under the door?

Problem Model 5

Bears had been selling so well that the store keeper put in a new order. She asked the bear factory to send twice the number of bears she already had on the shelves. How many did they send? How many did she have altogether?

123

THE TEDDY BEAR DELIVERIES PROBLEM MODELS (CONT.)

**Problem
Model 6**

The store is running low on white bears. They want a new delivery of half the number of bears currently on the shelves. How many will the factory need to send? How many white bears will they have altogether?

✪
**Problem
Model 7**

✪ It was the holiday season. Bears were selling like hotcakes. There were six bears on the shelves but an order went out for three more cases of bears. How many bears did the truck bring? How many did the store have in all?

124

THE TEDDY BEAR DELIVERIES PROBLEM MODELS (CONT.)

❂
**Problem
Model 8**

❂ There were nine bears on the store shelves.
The white bears were on the top shelf. The brown
bears were on the second shelf. There was one
more brown bear than white bear. How many
bears were on each shelf?

Crafting Story Problems

You will need...

- 9" x 12" pastel construction paper, 1 sheet per student, *or* The Teddy Bear Store storyboard, 1 copy per student, Blackline B99

- 4½" x 12" matching paper for story flaps, 1 per student*

- 2" x 2¾" pieces of construction paper, any color, for truck doors, 1 per student

- assorted cut pieces of construction paper for children to make store workers and truck drivers

- "mini curls" fake hair, available at many craft and fabric stores (optional)

- 2" x 2" pieces of brown and white construction paper from which to "hole punch" bear ears

- precut brown and white construction paper beans for bear faces

- teddy bear crates to share, 7 of each color per student, Blackline B114

- white construction paper in various sizes to make "talking bubbles"

- 3" x 6" brown construction paper for store counters, 1 per student*

- ¼" x 6" strips of brown construction paper for store shelves, 4 per student*

- 4$\frac{1}{2}$" x 6" bright colored pieces of construction paper for teddy bear trucks, 1 per student*
- 2" x 4$\frac{1}{2}$" pieces of black construction paper for truck wheels, 1 per student*
- student writing paper and pencils
- hole punchers to share (for ears)
- scissors, glue, crayons, and marking pens to share

*Note: The child who created the problem shown below started with blank paper and created his own construction paper truck and shop clerk while using precut construction paper shelves and bear faces. Some teachers prefer to have their students start with copies of The Teddy Bear Store storyboard blackline instead. These children glue on precut lima bean shapes for bear faces and draw or cut out paper workers. All they have to do for their trucks and shelves is to color their boards. While it's definitely easier that way, it's not as charming as having them work from scratch. If you decide to have children create their story problems from scratch, you'll need the items marked with asterisks (*) above, **in addition to** the other materials listed.*

Once all the problem models have been examined and solved, display them where children can easily refer to each kind as they create their own problems for others to solve.

Explain that you want each child to prepare a teddy bear store story problem to pose to the rest of the class (and perhaps to share with another class). You may or may not want to limit the number of bears children can use in their problems. We chose not to set limits this time around, but watched with interest as children found their own levels of comfort. It is important that the picture portion pose the problem as clearly as possible and the written portion support the picture with all needed details. Most children will want to begin with the picture part of their problem and may need another day before they're able to complete the written part. If this is the first time you're asking first graders to write the story portions of their problems, you'll need to model that step after the children complete their picture.

Teacher: Let's take a look at Steven's picture. What do you think he wants you to figure out?

Children: Oh, oh! He's only got ears on the shelves. Do we have to figure out how many bears?

Steven: That's it. See (pointing). There are two ears here for every bear.

Teacher: I want each of you to write the story part of your problem this time. How could Steven put his problem into words?

Children: He could say the bears were hiding. He could say all you can see are the bears' ears. He needs to say how many ears. He needs to ask how many bears. Then people will know what to figure out.

Teacher: You're very good helpers. Once Steven finishes writing his problem, I want him to read it to a friend and ask his friend if it makes sense. When he's made any needed corrections, he'll bring it to me so I can get it typed tonight. Tomorrow, he'll glue it to a story flap so everyone will be able to read it.

When both portions of children's story problems are complete, encourage them to check with classmates to see if their problems are clearly illustrated and written so others will understand what needs to be solved. Be sure to remind your students that each problem must be one that can be solved by their peers. Finally, have youngsters meet with you for final editing as needed.

That evening, if possible, type or print each child's problem on a 3$\frac{1}{2}$" x 11" strip of white paper, using standard spelling and punctuation. Since we both have Macintosh computers, we like to use a bold 36 point font with a sideways page set-up. That way we can type the whole batch of story problems at once, print them out, and cut them apart. Most computers have a 24 point font, if not a 36, but if you don't have access to a computer, you can print children's problems with wide-tip black felt marker. The point is to wind up with good quality print large enough to be read at a distance.

The next day, have children tape their story flaps to the picture portions of their story problems along the bottom. If they worked from scratch, using construction paper instead of blackline copies of the storyboard, they'll need

127

to glue their typed or printed strips to the 4¹/₂" x 12" strips of construction paper you precut in preparation for this activity and then tape the flaps to their pictures along the bottom.

Also, have each child glue the draft copy of his or her writing to the back of his or her picture—incorporating the rough draft into a finished product validates children's hard work and can be a nice source of information about students' growing capabilities in the areas of writing and spelling.

The lady only had four bears but she wanted twenty-four bears. How many bears will the truck need to bring?
by Kristen

the latye oNAly hAD 4 BArse BAtte SHe WaNtiD 24 BArse HaWe MiNe Wil thethnak neD to BeiNg Kristen.†

Solving Student Problems

Once children have completed their own story problems, it's sharing time. If they have been creating story problems all year, most of your second graders and some of your first graders will have become increasingly aware of their audience, and this is the ultimate test.

It will not be possible to have your students solve all their classmates' problems in one, or even two, sessions. We usually select four or five particularly interesting, unique, or challenging student problems for presentation to the group. As in previous sessions, children are seated on the rug with easy access to problem-solving materials.

You will need...

• student problems, select 4 or more

• a sheet of 8¹/₂" x 14" paper for each student (Show children how to fold their paper in fourths, so they can use it to show strategies and solutions for up to 8 problems.)

• pencils with erasers

- chalkboards to serve as hard writing surfaces if you're able to gather your children into a group meeting area on the rug
- The Teddy Bear Store storyboards, teddy bear counters, and teddy bear crates (Set these materials out in such a way that students who wish to use them can. Some children may prefer to work without them.)

This late in the year, we require first and second graders alike to set down their strategies and solutions on paper *before* we do much discussion. As we move through each problem, some children work mentally and record their thinking in numbers and/or words. It's very common for these students to illustrate their thinking in pictures as well. Some children use sketches or diagrams to solve problems, sometimes labeling their work with words or giving some sort of brief written explanation. Still others use manipulatives (even their fingers) and recreate their work in drawn or written form on the paper.

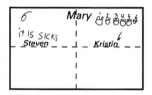

Before you pose the first student problem, have each child fold a piece of 8½" x 14" paper into four sections and write his or her name at the top. If you did the Presents theme last month, children will already be familiar with this routine. After children have set up their papers, present one problem at a time (or have the student author present it), allow time for questions or clarification, and have students spend some time working on their own at the rug. Expect some amount of interchange, especially among first graders, and plenty of looking around and imitation on the part of those who don't quite "get it". After a few minutes, ask those who are willing to share their solutions and explain their strategies.

First Grade Teacher: What do you notice about Steven's problem?

Children: He didn't make a truck. Those are ears. That's the one we helped him write. We have to figure out how many bears.

Steven: That's it—how many bears?

Teacher: Steven, would you like to read the story flap to the kids so they can hear what your question is?

Steven: Sure!

The store man can see twelve ears. How many bears are hiding?

Children: That's easy—all you have to do is count the ears.

Teacher: It sounds like some of you already have ideas about how to solve this problem. See if you can show your thinking on paper in drawings, numbers, or words so other people will understand how you're figuring it out.

After working for a minute or two, most of these first graders agreed that the answer to Steven's problem was six bears. Although this was the first time we'd asked them to show their thinking on paper *before* discussing solution ideas, many were able to respond in pictures or numbers.

Neal's approach to Steven's problem was to draw the ears and then assign one bear to each pair of ears. In looking at Neal's written responses over time, it was apparent that he had no limit to the paths he took toward solutions—drawings, counting patterns, number sentences, and tallying were just a few.

Brandon drew bear heads, each with two ears, until he had a total of twelve ears. He then numbered the bears and wrote six under them. Brandon often included drawings in his written responses. In other problem solutions, the drawing seemed to be included to validate a number sentence or a counting pattern he had tried earlier.

Neal's solution

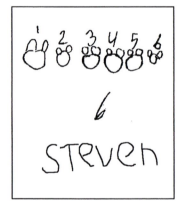

Brandon's solution

Kylie was one of the youngest children in the class. She seemed to have a variety of mental math strategies, but she often chose to write the answer in numbers and/or words. She always worked quickly and confidently.

Jessica's solution began with a drawing. Then she tried to write a number sentence about cutting the twelve in half but couldn't get it the way she wanted, so she crossed it out and wrote the six. She explained the $12 - 6$ was like using only half the ears to figure out the number of bears. Jessica's other written responses confirmed that she was eager to show her thinking in several ways, usually ending with a number sentence.

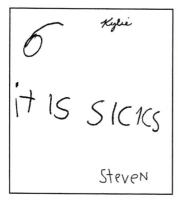

Kylie's solution

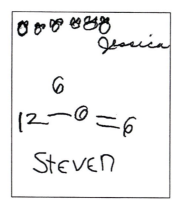

Jessica's solution

Plan to go through four or more student problems in the first sharing session. You will probably want to save samples of children's written responses to classmates' story problems, both to get a sense of the various strategies your entire group is using to solve different kinds of problems and also to characterize individuals' strategies or specific math skills.

While it's important to acknowledge each child's story problem, it's difficult to get through more than eight to ten even in two class sharing sessions. Here are some suggestions for honoring story problems not featured in class sharing sessions:

• Post the entire collection on one of your classroom walls after the first few have been shared with the class. Admire and read a few daily with your class.

• Post the collection in a display area outside the classroom. We have frequently seen children from other classrooms stop and try to figure out problems written by their friends.

• Work the more challenging problems together during one or two sharing sessions and save the rest to serve as "sponge activities". Many of the problems our students pose can be solved mentally and make wonderful two- or three-minute fillers before lunch or recess.

• Bind the story problems into mini-books to be enjoyed during math or reading time.

• Give the entire set to another class to work. A teacher participating in such a trade might review the collection, assign one problem to each of his or her students, and ask each student to supply an answer and a written explanation of how the answer was obtained. Your students will be thrilled to get their problems back, interested not only in whether or not the other children "got the right answer", but how they got their answers. (This particular suggestion works better with second graders than first.) Illustration on following page.

A mom walked into a store and she had 4 kids. She wanted to buy 5 bears for each kid. All the bears were $2.00 each. How much money did she spend? Jacob

• Send collections of student problems home for homework. In first grade, we make reduced copies of four student problems per week. We mount them two per sheet and make sure that we "publish" at least one problem from each student over the course of the year (see page 66). In second grade, we type the entire collection and ask our students to select ten to twelve to work and return.

Math Homework - Week of January 24-28

Please do at least ten of the teddy bear story problems in this collection. (You're welcome to do more, of course.) These are the problems your friends wrote last week and some of them are pretty hard. Be sure to show your thinking in words, numbers, or diagrams; if you only show the answer, I won't know how you solved each problem.

A mom walked into the store and the store had 20 bears. The mom had 5 kids. How many bears could the kids each have if the mom bought all the bears?

Breanna

There were 100 bears in the truck. The company had counted one of the bears twice. How many bears were there really?

Brenton

A mom walked into a store and she had 4 kids. She wanted to buy 5 bears for each kid. All the bears were $2.00 each. How much money did she spend?

Jacob

II: Buying & Selling Teddy Bears

Getting Started

ADDITION, SUBTRACTION, MULTIPLICATION & DIVISION

You will need...

• a sign that shows the bears are on sale: brown bears $5.00 each; white bears, $4.00 each; Blackline 115

• teddy bear counters, p. 185

• pretend bills in denominations of $1, $5, and $10, Blackline 126

• Unifix cubes or 1" square tiles

• paper, pencils, crayons

• chalkboards to serve as hard writing surfaces if you're able to gather your students into a group meeting area on the rug

When we first began working with the problems in this section, we simply let the children use paper money and other materials to "have at it". As usual, some of our students used diagrams, fingers, or other manipulatives, while others worked mentally, recording their thoughts with numbers or pictures.

The first several problems were relatively easy for most of our students but the last three posed substantial challenges to all. When a few finished before their classmates, we gave them different sums of money to spend and challenged them to continue working or, in some cases, to help other youngsters. Once again, we solicited explanations and demonstrations from students, which seemed to help some of the youngsters who needed extra support. The problems below (and variations of them) lasted over several days. With time, nearly every child was able to solve at least half the problems.

....

Addition / Multiplication

● The bears were on sale! Brown bears were $5.00 each, white bears were $4.00 each. Michael bought two brown bears and one white bear. How much did he spend?

Teacher: I see some of you have found ways to figure this one out. Can you tell us how you're working?

Brandon: I got some of those dollars and my bears. I put out five dollars for one brown bear, then five dollars for another brown bear, and then I put out four dollars for the white bear. I got five, ten, eleven, twelve, thirteen, fourteen dollars.

Teacher: Did anyone have a different way?

Rutta: I got some Unifix cubes. I put four together for a white bear and I set them beside one of my bears. Then I did five and five and put those beside two brown bears. That made ten and four more was fourteen. Fourteen dollars!

Andrew: I just wrote five and five are ten and then four more makes fourteen.

Johnny: I drew a picture of one white bear and I drew four dollars. Then I drew two brown bears and I'm still drawing five dollars for each of them.

Teacher: Those are all good ways of solving the problem. Those of you who are having difficulty getting started might want to move your work closer to someone who is feeling confident.

....

Addition / Multiplication (continued)

● Faith purchased three brown bears. They were on sale for $5.00 each. How much did she spend?

● The grandfather purchased four white bears for his grandchildren. Each was on sale for $4.00. How much did he spend?

✪ The school principal wanted to furnish each one of her classrooms with a teddy bear. She bought thirteen brown bears at $5.00 apiece. How much did she spend?

....

Division: Grouping / Sharing

● Dad had been to the big bear sale and brought home eleven bears for his three children to share evenly amongst themselves. How many bears did each child get?

✪ Grandma came into the store and bought sixteen bears. She wanted to give two of the bears to each of her grandchildren. How many grandchildren did she have?

● Cory came into the bear store with $17.00 to spend. He was very happy when he found out the bears were on sale. What could he buy?

Kristen: Wait a minute! That's tricky. Do we have to spend all of it?

Teacher: Is it possible to spend all of it?

Lisa: I think I can buy four white bears. See. Then I'd have one dollar left.

Cory: I'm trying it another way. Just a minute. Oops. I've got two dollars left over. Do we have to use all of it?

Jessica: I think I've got it. If you buy three white bears, that costs twelve dollars. Then you buy one brown bear. That costs five dollars. I spent all seventeen dollars.

Teacher: Great job all of you. Did anybody find a different way?

....

Division: Grouping / Sharing (continued)

● Jessica spent $28.00 at the bear store. Some of the bears she bought were brown, some were white. How many of each do you think she might have purchased?

✪ The preschool teacher had $40.00 to spend for new bears. He heard there was a great sale at the bear store. He couldn't decide whether to get all brown bears or all white bears or some of each. What could $40.00 buy? What do you think the best deal would be?

135

Creating Story Problems

Since this is the first time your children may have encountered money in the context of story problems we recommend that you continue to present problem models for students to examine, solve, and refer to in their own work. The models you present will give some youngsters an opportunity to challenge their classmates with very open ended or complex problems, while giving others permission to work at an easier level. You'll find that most of your children will design problems at their own mathematical comfort level.

EXAMINING SOME POSSIBILITIES

You will need...

- Buying and Selling Teddy Bears problem models, Blacklines B108-B112 and B123-B125

- a variety of problem-solving tools, including pretend bills in denominations of $1, $5, and $10, Unifix cubes, scratch paper and pencils

Begin by asking children to examine the picture portion of one of your problem models. Can they figure out what the problem is by looking at the picture alone? Show them the story problem on the flap. Does the story help to clarify the problem to be solved? Once they've determined what the problem is, ask them to work toward a solution, either mentally or by using any of the tools you've provided. Continue in this fashion until you've worked your way through the entire collection of problem models.

BUYING AND SELLING TEDDY BEARS PROBLEM MODELS

To make copies of these problem models for use in your own classroom, see Blacklines B109-B112 and B123-125.

Problem Model 9

Grandma had four wonderful grandchildren. She wanted to buy two bears for each one. How many did she need to buy? How many bears did the store have left?

Problem Model 10

A little girl bought two brown bears at $5.00 each and two white bears at $4.00 each to decorate her room. How much did she have to pay in all?

BUYING AND SELLING PROBLEM MODELS (CONT.)

**Problem
Model 11**

Grandpa bought nine teddy bears, planning to
give three of them to each of his grandchildren.
How many grandchildren did he have?

**Problem
Model 12**

Johnny had been saving his money. He had $19
and wanted to buy some new teddy bears. He
went to the corner bear store where brown bears
cost $5 each and white bears cost $4 each. What
was he able to buy?

138

BUYING AND SELLING PROBLEM MODELS (CONT.)

✪
**Problem
Model 13**

✪ **Damon had $12.00 to spend at the Teddy Bear Store. He found bears priced at $3.00. $4.00, $5.00, $6.00, and $7.00. Which bears was he able to buy?**

Crafting Story Problems

You will need...

- 9" x 12" pastel construction paper, 1 sheet per student *or* The Teddy Bear Store storyboard (without the truck), 1 copy per student, Blackline B99

- 4¹/₂" x 12" matching construction paper for story problem flaps, 1 per student*

- assorted cut pieces of construction paper for children to make store clerks and shoppers

- craft "mini curls" fake hair (optional but quite charming)

- 2" x 2" pieces of brown and white construction paper from which to "hole punch" bear ears

- precut brown and white construction paper "beans" for bear faces

- paper money in all three denominations, see Blacklines

- white construction paper in various sizes to make "talking bubbles" for question marks, words, and numbers that signal the problems to be solved

- 3" x 6" brown construction paper for store counter, 1 per student*

- ¹/₄" x 6" strips of brown construction paper for store shelves, 4 per student*

- student writing paper and pencils

- hole punchers to share (for ears)
- scissors, glue, crayons, and marking pens to share

Note: Because the problems in this section involve buying and selling teddy bears, rather than teddy bear delivery, there is no truck associated with any of the models. You can run a blackline copy of The Teddy Bear Store storyboard, cut off the truck and reproduce copies of the shelf section as shown in the problem below, or just have children make their own story problems from scratch, using your problem models for reference. You'll need the items with asterisks (*) above, in addition to the other materials listed if you decide to have children create their story problems from scratch.

When all the problem models have been examined and solved, display them where children can easily refer to each kind as they create their own problems for others to solve. For further details about helping students produce their own story problems, please see Crafting Story Problems earlier in this chapter, pages 125-128.

The Teddy Bear Store had 6 bears on sale and 14 not on sale. Which bears can this lady buy? She has $40.00.

Faith

Solving Student Problems

You will need...

- student problems, select 4 or more
- 8½" x 14" paper, 1 sheet per student
- pencils with erasers
- chalkboards to serve as hard writing surfaces if you're able to gather your children into a group meeting area on the rug

- pretend bills in denominations of $1, $5, and $10
- Unifix cubes or 1" square tiles; you might also make base ten pieces and calculators available to your second graders if they have used very large numbers in their story problems

Once children have completed their own story problems, choose four or five of the more interesting, unique, or challenging student stories for presentation to the group. Gather your students in a central location, if possible, and distribute paper, pencils, and chalkboards for writing surfaces. Keep other problem-solving materials within easy reach, and let the sharing begin.

Second Grade Teacher: This is Sara's Teddy Bear story problem. Can you tell what it is she wants you to figure out just by looking at her picture?

A Teddy Bear Problem

One day the Teddy Bear Store had 25 bears. A mom walked in and said, "I need 25 bears and I have 8 children. But I don't know how many they each get."

Sara

Children: There's a lady with a bag in her hand. It looks like she's buying something. The bubble over her head says, "Eight children, how many bears?" You mean, how many bears for each kid? I don't get it. How are we supposed to figure that out? How many bears is she going to buy? If she buys eight, they can each have one. Is she going to buy more than eight?

Sara: I'll read the problem to you. Then you'll know what to do. But I picked hard numbers, so it's not going to be easy!

One day the Teddy Bear Store had 25 bears. A mom walked in and said, "I need 25 bears and I have 8 children. But I don't know how many they each get."

141

Children: A mom with 8 kids! That's a lot! No wonder she has to buy so many bears! They'll each get more than one if the mom's going to buy twenty-five.

Teacher: This is an interesting problem. Why don't you start working and see what you come up with?

Although the answer to this problem was not immediately obvious to any of our second graders, most concluded that the answer was three bears per child with one left over. The most common strategy was to draw eight circles to represent the eight kids and then to apportion the twenty-five bears evenly among the circles by means of lines or dots:

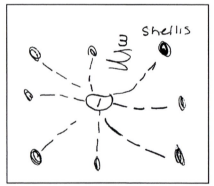
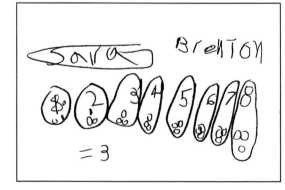

Ryan, who'd worked the problem the day before, decided to have a bit of fun with the leftover bear and wrote:

The answer is 3 and $\frac{1}{8}$: 3 + 3 + 3 + 3 + 3 + 3 + 3 + 3 = 24; there will be one bear left! We have to cut that one in eight pieces. The kids are screaming, "I want the eye!" "I want the mouth!"

III: Graphing Teddy Bear Sales

You will need...

- overhead(s) of the Bear Store Sales graph(s), Blacklines B116-B117
- Vis-á-Vis pen
- an overhead calculator if you have one and plan to have students use calculators
- student calculators to share
- Bear Store Sales graphs you plan to use, 1 copy of each per student, Blacklines B116-B117

In this section, you will find graphing problems, posed at two different levels of difficulty. The first graph asks children to chart daily sales of teddy bears. We've provided the sales figures and structured the graph in such a way that children can represent one bear sale with one box. The challenge lies in comparing quantities sold each day and figuring out total sales for the week. The second also asks children to chart daily sales, but does not provide enough boxes to accommodate the numbers given. Children must figure out how to construct the graph before they compare and total the sales figures.

Display a transparency of Bear Store Sales Graph No. 1 on the overhead, discuss it briefly, and let the children go to work. Even though it is relatively straightforward, we recommend that second grade teachers use it to set the stage for the second sales graph.

Bear Store Sales   Graph No. 1

On Monday, the bear store sold 15 bears. Tuesday, they sold 10 bears. On Wednesday, they sold 5 bears. On Thursday, they sold 10 bears. On Friday, they sold 15 bears. Create a graph to show the bear sales for the week.

Mon.															
Tues.															
Wed.															
Thurs.															
Fri.															

1. Which day did the store sell the fewest bears? _____

2. Did they sell more bears on Monday or Tuesday? _____

   How many more? _____

3. How many bears did the store sell in all? _____

Teacher: Let's read the top portion of the graphing sheet together and see if we can figure out what to do.

Children: It's sort of like some of the other graphs we've made this year. The kind we put on the wall. Like the one about what color we wanted our hats to be. And the weather graph on the calendar. And the kind about how far our toy cars would roll. We made one to show how many paper clips our magnets would hold too.

Teacher: Good for you! You remember many of the graphs we've already done this year. Please help me read the information here at the top.

(The information is read together.)

Children: That's a lot of bears. Look, it has the days by the boxes.

Teacher: How could you represent the bear sales for each day on this grid?

Children: Could we color in a box for each bear that was sold? Or even draw a bear in each box? Maybe we could draw a line with a crayon across as many boxes as the bears that got sold that day. Maybe we could write a number in each box. Like one, two, three, up to fifteen for Monday.

Teacher: I think those all sound like good ideas. Let's take a look at the questions on the bottom of the paper. How could you figure those out?

Children: I can't read them. Me either. I can!

Teacher: Let's read them together.

Children: Does fewest mean not very many? They sold fifteen on Monday. That's not the littlest. They sold just ten on Tuesday. We need to color the graph before we can do those questions.

Teacher: I think that might help you a lot. What if someone needs help reading a question?

Children: I could help. Me too. They could ask you. Lots of us could help.

Teacher: What if someone can't figure out how many bears the store sold altogether?

Children: Could we get the calculator? We could just count. We could count the boxes by fives.

Teacher: It sounds like you'll be able to do a fine job together.

The next day, display the second Bear Store Sales graph on the overhead. This graph offers a different sort of challenge, in that there are not enough boxes to designate one per bear. Our second graders were most intrigued with this problem and had an interesting discussion about how to represent the bears on the grid.

---

name _____

Bear Store Sales   Graph No. 2

On Monday, the bear store sold 30 bears. Tuesday, they sold 20 bears. On Wednesday, they sold 35 bears. On Thursday, they sold 25 bears. On Friday, they sold 15 bears.

Create a graph to show the bear sales for the week.

On which day did the store sell the most bears? _____

On which day did the store sell the fewest bears? _____

Did they sell more bears on Monday or Tuesday? _____

How many more? _____

Did they sell fewer bears on Tuesday or Wednesday?

How many fewer? _____

How many bears did the store sell in all? _____

Teacher: What do you notice about today's graph?

Children: It talks about days at the top of the sheet, but the graph doesn't have the names of the days beside it. It's about bears again. More bears this time—they sold thirty on Monday!

Teacher: Where would you enter that information on this empty grid? How could you set it up to show that the store sold thirty bears on Monday?

Breanna: We could put Monday's bears across the top row of boxes, just like yesterday's graph.

Michael: It won't work. There aren't thirty boxes. Maybe we could get some more graph paper and tape it on.

Johnny: We could just tape a bunch of those sheets together.

Teacher: That's true. You could tape on more paper to make thirty boxes across. Does anyone have a different idea?

145

Laura: What if we used the boxes to count by fives. I mean, what if each box was like five bears instead of one bear?

Natasha: That would work! Look—five, ten, fifteen, twenty, twenty-five, thirty—you'd only need six boxes for Monday.

Brenton: We could say that each box was for three bears. We could even draw three dots in each box.

Teacher: How would you show the twenty bears that got sold on Tuesday?

Brenton: Three, six, nine, twelve, fifteen, eighteen, hmmm...it doesn't land on twenty when you count by threes.

Kaylyn: What about tens? You could go by tens!

Teacher: How would you show Wednesday's sales? They sold thirty-five bears that day.

Kaylyn: I know! You could use half a box. That's what I'm going to do. I'll use boxes for tens and color in just half a box if I need five!

Teacher: It sounds like many of you have some interesting ideas about how you're going to handle this challenge. I have only one more question before you go off to work. If Laura says each box on her graph means five bears, and Brenton says every box means three, and Kaylyn says each box means ten, how will someone else know what each box means?

Marco: Write it at the top. It could be like a map key, you know. You could draw a little picture of a box and put the number you wanted beside it.

Teacher: That would be one way to handle it.

The Cookie Store

The Cookie Store

L ike The Teddy Bear Store, this theme is divided into three parts: Baking Cookies, Buying and Selling Cookies, and Graphing Cookie Sales. The problems in Part I revisit every whole number operation already introduced, with a new twist—thinking in terms of dozens and half dozens. To children accustomed to working in tens, fives, and ones, this presents new and interesting challenges. A simple addition problem, for instance, takes on an extra step as children figure out how many cookies there are in half a dozen:

The cookie store had only a half dozen peanut butter cookies and four chocolate chip cookies left after a busy day. How many cookies did it have in all?

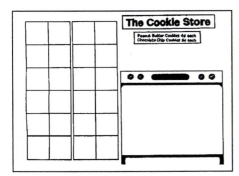

The structure of the storyboard, which shows two cookie sheets each divided into twelve equal sections beside an oven, helps many children solve these problems.

Devote a week or more to Part I. Pose the suggested problems in oral and written form, then have your students de-

147

velop their own story problems. Return to the Cookie Store theme a month later to work on Part II, which involves money. In this section, we extend the challenges introduced in the Teddy Bear Store unit, posing such problems as:

> A college student came and bought four chocolate chip cookies at 5¢ each. How much did she have to pay?

> A man came into a cookie store where peanut butter cookies cost 4¢ each and chocolate chip cookies cost 5¢ each. He had 29¢ to spend and left without any change. What could he have purchased? Is there more than one solution to this problem?

> The teacher wanted nine peanut butter cookies at 4¢ apiece. She gave the clerk two quarters. How much change should she get?

Because we're using coins instead of dollar bills this time, children are challenged to think in chunks of fives, tens, and twenty-fives as they count sums of money and make change. Devote another week, perhaps a little longer, to the problems in Part II. Pose suggested story problems orally and in written form, and then have children create their own. The graphing problems in Part III take no more than two or three days and offer closure on the theme of buying and selling cookies.

HOW IT WORKED FOR US

After watching our children's growth with the teddy bear story problems, we decided to forge ahead with The Cookie Store. Could our children relate their growing confidence with fives and tens to half dozens and dozens? Could they compute cookie purchases and figure out simple change? Was this a good place for partners to combine their counters to work with larger numbers?

We knew that our students had many informal ways of dealing with such operations as comparing, multiplication, and division. Would calculators be of any help to them in their attempts to solve larger problems? Would they know what keys to push? Would their interest in using calculators help them understand formal symbolization or enhance their sense of number operations in any way?

We decided our children had experienced enough secret doors to last a lifetime and we designed a no-frills story board that showed only two cookie trays, each subdivided into twelve equal boxes. Our double cookie tray problems were successful for second graders. However, our first graders showed us just how fragile their foundations were and how many times they needed to experience big ideas in familiar settings. Though most of them dutifully worked their way through our double tray problems, the earlier joy the secret door had provided seemed to be missing this time. Back to the drawing board. We needed a secret door—an oven door? It was amazing how magical the new problems became with that added door.

This late in the year, we assumed our students would be at ease with money—and the second graders were. Our first graders surprised us, however. Never did we expect some of them to ask what those big and little silver coins were called, and how much each was worth. After all, they'd worked with money many times and, in our judgment, seemed to be fairly competent.

Ah, humility! New challenges can do funny things to such young learners. So we started over at an easier level, helping children count out appropriate coins for one chocolate chip cookie and one peanut butter cookie, then two of each, before posing more challenging problems involving money. The children's confidence returned along with increased risk-taking.

The graphs proved to be another enlightening experience. As long as there was one-to-one correspondence between the cookies sold and the boxes on the graphing sheet, no one had much trouble. Even designating one graphing box per dozen cookies wasn't too difficult for most of our second graders when they were asked to compare quantities and report how many cookies were sold in any given day. Many were even able to compute the week's total cookie sales with the help of a calculator.

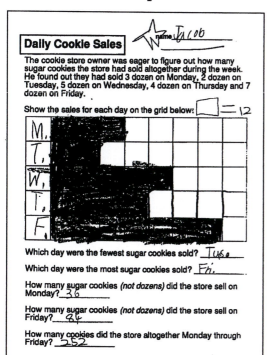

Challenging them to compute how much *money* the store made over a five-day period when sales for each day were represented in dozens proved to be too difficult, however, even for the most able students. It was May and they were sure they could handle almost anything. Their sales totals ranged from $1.34 to $60,000.00 and, in the end, they advised us to scrap that particular problem, donating it, perhaps, to the third or fourth graders up the hall. We were reminded that even our seven- and eight-year-olds had their limits when it came to being able to work with large numbers.

I: Baking Cookies

Getting Started

ADDITION, SUBTRACTION, MULTIPLICATION & DIVISION

You will need...

- overhead of The Cookie Store storyboard, Blackline 127
- overhead cookies, 2 dozen: 12 "peanut butter" & 12 "chocolate chip", Blackline B1
- calculators, a half class set for children to share
- The Cookie Store storyboard, 1 copy per student, Blackline 127
- Baker's Dough cookies, 2 dozen per student: 12 "peanut butter" and 12 "chocolate chip", pp. 186-187

Begin the new theme by posing problems and asking children to work with their storyboards and cookies. Don't insist that students show their solutions with cookies on their boards if they can solve the problems by looking at the empty cookie tray frames or by using mental arithmetic.

Some students enjoy using calculators if you make them available, although their informal methods of solving certain problems won't always translate directly to the calculator keys. We find that if children work in partners, using storyboards and cookies in combination with calculators, they're sometimes able to figure a solution with manipulatives first and work backwards to a number sentence on the calculator that will show the correct answer. In this way, calculators can become tools for teaching standard notation. If you allow children to struggle a bit, you'll also find they begin to make judgments about the most effective use of calculators, realizing that sometimes a visual or mental solution is faster or easier.

As your students solve the problems, encourage children to share the different strategies they're trying. It will probably take two or three class sessions to cover this set of problems and second grade teachers may want to leave out some of the easier examples and feature those with stars.

....

How Many Altogether?

● The cookie store had only a half dozen peanut butter cookies and four chocolate chip cookies left after a busy day. How many cookies did they have in all?

● There were two half-full trays of chocolate chip cookies at the end of the day. How many cookies were there in all?

How Many Are Left?

● It was nearly closing time. The cookie store had only eleven cookies in stock. A little boy rushed in and bought five. How many cookies were left?

✪ It was nearly closing time. The cookie store had twenty-three cookies in stock. A man rushed in to buy fourteen for his family. How many cookies were left?

Missing Addend / Missing Subtrahend

● The cookie maker was trying to fill an order for a dozen peanut butter cookies. She had five cooling on a tray while the rest were baking in the oven. How many were in the oven?

✪ The cookie store workers started the morning with two dozen cookies on hand. By the end of the morning they had nine cookies left. How many had they sold?

✪ There was a telephone order for two dozen peanut butter cookies. When the worker checked, he saw that the store had one full tray and another tray with only four cookies. How many more cookies would he need to make to fill the order?

Our second graders found the problem below particularly challenging, and some of them opted to share cookies and boards in order to have three dozen.

✪ The cookie store workers were hurrying to finish three dozen cookies. They had sixteen chocolate chip cookies and thirteen peanut butter cookies already cooling on the counter. The others were baking in the oven. How many of the three dozen were still in the oven?

Partitioning

● Dad decided to bake five cookies in the oven. Some of the cookies were chocolate chip, some were peanut butter. One more was chocolate chip than peanut butter. How many of each were baking?

✪ The cookie store workers had arrived early to make cookies. So far they had finished twelve cookies. Twice as many were peanut butter as chocolate chip. How many of each had they made?

✪ There were eighteen cookies on the trays, half as many chocolate chip cookies as peanut butter cookies. How many were there of each kind?

151

In the following problems, encourage children to continue working in partners, sharing cookies, boards, and calculators. Though each of the problems below could be solved via formal multiplication and division, you will see primary students pursue diverse strategies—counting out all the cookies; counting on their fingers; using repeated addition or subtraction; drawing to demonstrate doubling, cutting, sharing; and/or using mental math with verbal explanations.

Working With Dozens and Half Dozens

● The cookiemaker found two trays, each with a half dozen peanut butter cookies left from the evening before. There was a third tray with a half dozen chocolate chip cookies on it. How many day-old cookies did the store have in all?

✪ The store had one full tray of peanut butter cookies and one full tray of chocolate chip cookies. They also had a half dozen of each kind baking in the oven. How many were in the oven? How many cookies did they have in all?

Twice As Many

● The cookie maker had just set out four peanut butter cookies to cool. There were twice as many cookies in the oven. How many were in the oven? How many will there be altogether?

✪ The cookie maker had just finished making eleven cookies before she had to stop and write down some phone orders. The owner decided to help out and she made twice as many as the cookie maker had made. How many did the owner make? How many cookies in all?

Half As Many

✪ There were eighteen chocolate chip cookies and half as many peanut butter cookies on display. How many cookies altogether?

Division: Sharing / Grouping

● Six girls came in to the bakery and bought a dozen cookies to share. How many will each get to eat?

✪ Three children bought a dozen and a half cookies to share. How many will each get to eat?

✪ The cookie makers made forty-two cookies. How many trays did they need?

Creating Story Problems

Nearly all of your first and second graders will be able to write stories to accompany their picture problems by now. We still present models of story problems in picture and word form which children examine and solve. After working with our models, children go on to create their own problems. Some still modify our models only a little (usually making the numbers bigger) while others are able to invent their own pictorial, written, or mathematical twists. Once again, we find that most children tend to design problems at their own mathematical comfort level.

EXAMINING SOME POSSIBILITIES

You will need...

• Baking Cookies problem models, Blacklines B128-B132 and B138-B141

• calculators for students to share

• The Cookie Store storyboard, 1 copy per student, Blackline B127

• Baker's Dough cookies, 2 dozen per student

Begin by asking children to examine the picture portion of one of your problem models. Can they figure out what the problem is by looking at the picture alone? Show them the written story problem on the flap. Does the story help to clarify the problem to be solved?

Teacher: I've put together some new problem models for you to solve today. Although the written story problem is hidden behind this flap, I'm eager to know if you can figure out what the problem is just by looking at the picture.

Children: There's a question mark on the oven door so we have to figure out what's in there. There are seven cookies on his tray. There's a talking bubble—he wants to have twelve cookies. It's going to be five. I can tell because I counted the empty spaces on the tray. Not me, I thought of six and six—that makes twelve—then I said it would be five because six and one more made seven already on the tray.

Teacher: Great thinking and problem solving! Let's take a look at the written part of the problem.

The cookie maker needed one dozen chocolate chip cookies. He had seven on the tray and the rest were baking in the oven. How many were in the oven?

Children: We did it. We figured it out with just the picture.

Teacher: You did that very well. You've had a lot of practice this year. Do you think the story part might have helped a child from another class know what the problem was?

Children: They would know for sure if they read the story, but the picture would help a lot too.

Have students examine each of your problem models, discussing, reading and solving the problems as they go. We find that children often solve our picture/word problems mentally in the process of examining them, but they can certainly use the cookies and boards and/or calculators as well. Once all your problem models have been examined, display them in a prominent area at eye level so students can think about which they might like to copy or modify when they create their own story problems.

BAKING COOKIES PROBLEM MODELS

To make copies of these problem models for use in your own classroom, see Blacklines B128-B132 and B138-B141.

Problem Model 1

The cookie maker needed one dozen chocolate chip cookies. He had seven on the tray and the rest were baking in the oven. How many were in the oven?

BAKING COOKIES PROBLEM MODELS (CONT.)

Problem Model 2

The cookie maker had sixteen cookies cooling on the trays and half as many in the oven. How many were in the oven? How many did she have altogether?

Problem Model 3

The cookie maker has six peanut butter cookies on display and twice as many baking in the oven. How many are in the oven? How many will they have in all?

BAKING COOKIES PROBLEM MODELS (CONT.)

Problem Model 4

The cookie maker had nine cookies in the oven. There was one more chocolate chip cookie than peanut butter cookie. How many of each kind were in the oven?

✪
Problem Model 5

✪ The cookie maker had a dozen cookies in the oven. Twice as many of them were peanut butter cookies as chocolate chip cookies. How many of each kind were in the oven?

Crafting Story Problems

You will need...

- 9" x 12" white, manila, or pastel construction paper, 1 sheet per student, *or* The Cookie Store storyboard, 1 copy per student, Blackline B127

- 4¹⁄₂" x 12" matching construction paper for story flaps, 1 per student*

- 4" x 5" white construction paper for oven doors, 1 per student

- 3" x 9" strips of manila paper from which to cut cookies

- assorted cut pieces of construction paper for store workers

- "mini curls" fake hair, available at many craft and fabric stores (optional)

- white construction paper in various sizes to make "talking bubbles" for question marks, words, and numbers that signal the problems to be solved

- precut ovens, Blackline B144*

- precut large trays, Blackline B148*

- precut Cookie Store signs, Blackline B146*

- scissors, crayons, marking pens, scotch tape, and glue to share

- writing paper and pencils

She wants sixteen cookies. How many are in the oven?
by Eilbert

Note: The child, who created the problem shown here, started with blank paper and glued on an oven cutout and a tray, while drawing her own store worker. Some teachers prefer to have their students start with copies of The Cookie Store storyboard instead. Their children are able to simply tape precut paper oven doors onto the oven drawings and draw or glue on cookie cutouts and workers as they create their own story problems. While it's definitely easier that way, it's not as charming as having them work from scratch. If you decide to have children create their story problems from scratch, you'll need the items marked with asterisks (*) above, in addition to the other materials listed.

Once all your problem models have been examined and solved, display them where children can easily refer to each kind as they create their own problems for others to solve.

Explain that you want each child to prepare a story problem to pose to the rest of the class (and perhaps to share with another class). It is important that the picture portion pose the problem as clearly as possible and that the written portion support the picture with all needed details. Think again about whether or not you want to impose limits on the numbers of cookies children use in their story problems. We chose to let our students find their own comfort levels this time.

Most children will want to begin with the picture part of their problem and may need another day before they're able to complete the written part. Once both portions are complete, encourage children to check with classmates to see if their problems are clearly illustrated and written so others will understand what needs to be solved. Be sure to remind your students that each problem must be one that can be solved by their peers. Finally, have youngsters meet with you for final editing as needed.

That evening, if possible, type or print each child's problem on a 3½" x 11" strip of white paper, using standard spelling and punctuation. Since we both have Macintosh computers, we like to use a bold 36 point font with a sideways page set-up. That way we can type the whole batch of story problems at once, print them out, and cut them apart. Most computers have a 24 point font, if not a 36, but if you don't have access to a computer, you can print children's problems with wide-tip black felt marker. The point is to wind up with good quality print large enough to be read at a distance.

The next day, have children tape their story flaps to the picture portions of their story problems along the bottom. If they worked from scratch, using construction paper instead of blackline copies of the storyboard, they'll need to glue the typed or printed strips to the 4½" x 12" pieces of construction paper you precut in preparation for this activity and then tape the flaps to their pictures along the bottom.

The work lady made 31 cookies and she had a telephone call, and when she was on the telephone another lady went in and put some of the cookies in the oven. When she came back, she only saw 7 on the counter. How many are in the oven?

by Breanna

The work land made 31 cookie and She had a tallfn callde ~~and~~ and when she wos on the tallfn a nathr land wit in and put cookie in the avn. When she Kam bak she olny sol 7 on the canr. How many more is in the avn?

158

Also, have each child glue the draft copy of his or her writing to the back of his or her picture—incorporating the rough draft into the finished product validates children's hard work and can be a nice source of information about students' growing capabilities in the areas of writing and spelling.

Solving Student Problems

You will need...

- selected student problems

- half sheets of ditto paper *or* 8½" x 14" paper folded into quarters for each student

- pencils with erasers

- chalkboards to serve as hard writing surfaces, if you're able to gather your children into a group meeting area on the rug

- Unifix cubes or 1" square tiles, Baker's Dough cookies, Cookie Store storyboards, and calculators in an area easily accessible to children

additional materials for second graders:

- base ten pieces if student problems involve very large numbers

- typed half sheet copies of student story problems (or reduced copies of all the picture problems with story flaps showing) set out so children can select problems they will try to solve independently after the first whole-group sharing session

Once children have completed their own story problems, it's sharing time. If they have been creating story problems all year, most of your students will have become increasingly aware of their audience and this is the ultimate test. Not all the problems children have written can be solved. Even as we edit and type the final copy, we try not to interfere with a child's meaning and intent. If the problem cannot be solved as written, we wait for the class to help the author restructure it, encouraging children to be as supportive as possible in their suggestions.

Not all the children's problems can be shared in one, or even two class sessions. We usually select four or five particularly interesting, unique, or challenging student problems for presentation to the group. As in previous sessions, children are seated on the rug with easy access to problem-solving materials. This late in the year, we ask first and second graders alike to set down their strategies and solutions on paper prior to class discussion.

As we move through each problem, some children work mentally and record their thinking in numbers and/or words. It's very common for students to illustrate their thinking in pictures as well. Some children use sketches or diagrams to solve problems, sometimes labeling their work with

159

words or giving some sort of brief written explanation. Still others use manipulatives (other than their fingers) and recreate their work in drawn or written form on the paper.

Present one problem at a time (or have the student author present it), allow time for questions or clarification, and have children spend some time working on their own at the rug. Expect some amount of interchange among students, especially first graders, and plenty of looking around and imitation on the part of those who don't quite "get it". After a few minutes, ask those who are willing to share their solutions and explain their strategies.

Second Grade Teacher: Just looking at her picture, what do you notice about Emily's problem?

Children: It's beautiful! She must have spent a long time on her drawing. The lady by the counter is saying thirty-two, but there are only eight cookies on the counter. There's a question mark on the oven door, though. She must want us to figure out how many are in the oven. That's kind of hard. No, it isn't—it's easy!

Teacher: For some of you, this may seem easy and, for others, it may seem more difficult. Let's read the written part.

Two workers were in the kitchen. Tammy was thinking, "If there's supposed to be 32 cookies, how many did Mary put in the oven?"

Children: So she does want us to figure out how many are in the oven. I already know!

Teacher: Please take a few minutes to work Emily's problem on your own. If you already know the answer, your challenge will be to explain in words, numbers, or drawings how you figured it out. If you don't already know, you could...?

Children: Draw the cookies on the counter and then keep going 'til you get up to thirty-two. Not me! I'm going to write a subtraction sentence. I like to use tally marks.

Teacher: There are many ways to solve this problem. Why don't you go ahead and get your ideas down on paper?

In the course of discussing any particular problem, our students often proposed several different ways to figure out an answer. In this case, everyone agreed that the solution was twenty-four, and most were able to express their thinking rather clearly on paper.

Faith solved Emily's problem by means of a picture, first showing the eight cookies on the counter and then drawing cookies in the oven until she reached a total of thirty-two. She then went back and counted the cookies in the oven to determine that twenty-four were needed to reach a total of thirty-two.

Laura held the eight cookies in her head and counted on until she reached a total of thirty-two, using tally marks to keep track of her thinking. She then went back and counted her tally marks, arriving at an answer of twenty-four.

JoDell worked in a fashion very similar to Laura, holding the eight in her head and counting on until she reached thirty-two. She used her fingers at first and then showed her solution with tally marks, grouping them by tens and ones.

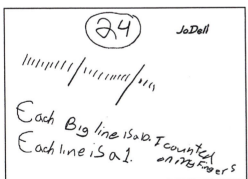

Timmy knew that thirty-two take away eight would give him the solution, so he simply recorded 32 – 8. His response didn't show how he figured the answer, but he usually worked in chunks, and probably took away two and then six more to arrive at twenty-four.

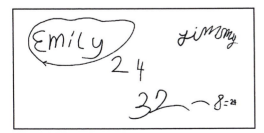

Danny
Emily

24+8=32
aT FirsT I
ThoT IT WaS
22 BuT IT WaS
noT So I aDiD
2 mor and
ThAT IeGLD 24
Then I aDd 2 mor and IrecLd
32

Danny started by thinking of a number that would combine with eight to give him thirty-two. As he explained it, he started with twenty-two, which must have seemed like a reasonable figure, and adjusted upward.

Plan to go through four or five student problems in the first sharing session. You may want to save samples of children's written responses to classmates' story problems, both to get a sense of the various strategies your entire group is using to solve different kinds of problems and also to characterize individuals' strategies or specific math skills.

While it's important to acknowledge each child's story problem, it's difficult to get through more than eight to ten, even in two class sharing sessions. Here are some suggestions for honoring the story problems not featured in class sharing sessions:

• Post the entire collection on the wall after the first few have been shared with the class. Admire and read a few daily with your students.

• Post the entire collection in a display area outside the classroom. We have frequently seen children from other classrooms stop and try to figure out problems written by their friends.

• Work the more challenging problems together during one or two sharing sessions and save the rest to serve as "sponge activities". Many of the problems that our students posed can be solved mentally and make wonderful two- or three-minute fillers before lunch or recess or at other times of transition.

• Bind the story problems into mini-books to be enjoyed during math or reading time.

• Second grade teachers: set out student problems in typed form (one problem per half page) or make reduced copies of the problems, with the story flaps showing. Have children select problems of their own choosing and work them independently. Ask that they show their thinking in drawings, numbers, and/or words—let them know that an answer is not enough.

• Give the entire set to another class to work. A teacher participating in such a trade might review the collection, assign one problem to each of his or her students, and ask each child to supply an answer and a written explanation of how the answer was obtained. Your students will be thrilled to get their problems back, interested not only in whether the other children "got the right answer", but how they got their answers. (This particular suggestion works better with second graders than first.)

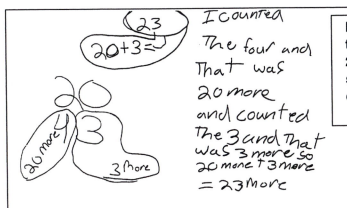

I counted
The four and
That was
20 more
and counted
The 3 and That
was 3 more so
20 more + 3 more
= 23 more

20 more 43 3 More

23
20+3=

How many more are on the counter? She had 20 inside the oven and she had 43 on the counter.
by Clara

• Send collections of student problems home for homework. In first grade, we make reduced copies of four to six student problems per week. We mount them two per sheet and make sure that we "publish" at least one problem from each student over the course of the year. In second grade, we type the entire collection and ask our students to select ten to twelve to work and return.

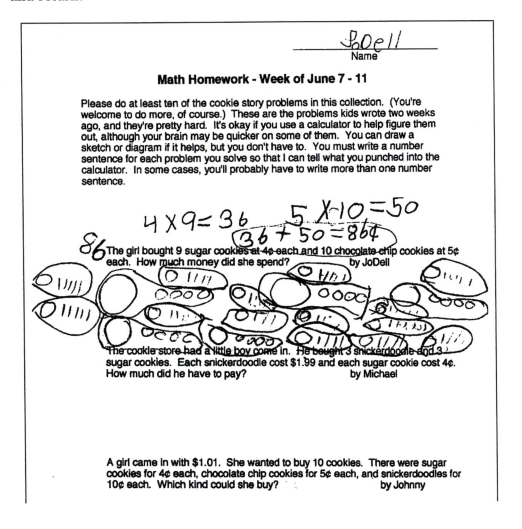

JoDell
Name

Math Homework - Week of June 7 - 11

Please do at least ten of the cookie story problems in this collection. (You're welcome to do more, of course.) These are the problems kids wrote two weeks ago, and they're pretty hard. It's okay if you use a calculator to help figure them out, although your brain may be quicker on some of them. You can draw a sketch or diagram if it helps, but you don't have to. You must write a number sentence for each problem you solve so that I can tell what you punched into the calculator. In some cases, you'll probably have to write more than one number sentence.

$4 \times 9 = 36$ $5 \times 10 = 50$
$36 + 50 = 86$ ¢

86 The girl bought 9 sugar cookies at 4¢ each and 10 chocolate chip cookies at 5¢ each. How much money did she spend?   by JoDell

The cookie store had a little boy come in. He bought 3 snickerdoodle and 3 sugar cookies. Each snickerdoodle cost $1.99 and each sugar cookie cost 4¢. How much did he have to pay?   by Michael

A girl came in with $1.01. She wanted to buy 10 cookies. There were sugar cookies for 4¢ each, chocolate chip cookies for 5¢ each, and snickerdoodles for 10¢ each. Which kind could she buy?   by Johnny

163

II: Buying & Selling Cookies
Getting Started

ADDITION, SUBTRACTION, MULTIPLICATION & DIVISION

You will need...

- a large sign: Peanut Butter Cookies 4¢ each, Chocolate Chip Cookies 5¢ each, Blackline B145
- a variety of problem-solving tools, including ziplock bags of change (4 dimes, 4 nickels, 15 pennies per bag for first graders; 4 dimes, 4 nickels, 30 pennies, 2 quarters per bag for second graders), Unifix cubes, scratch paper and pencils, and calculators

In Part II of The Cookie Store theme, we extend the challenges introduced in The Teddy Bear Store, using coins instead of dollar bills. Children are challenged to think in chunks of fives, tens, and twenty-fives as they figure costs, count sums of money, and make change. As in the Teddy Bear Store, we've posed some problems that have several different solutions, such as:

> A teacher stopped in to buy some cookies. Chocolate chip cookies cost 5¢ and sugar cookies cost 4¢. She gave the clerk a quarter and got a nickel back. What could she have bought?

Even if your students struggled with such problems the first time around, don't hesitate to have another go. We were often surprised at our students' willingness to "try those hard ones again." Your first graders may need a lot of support in the beginning. Don't be surprised if you hear:

What's this one (coin) called?

How many pennies are in this kind?

Is the big silver one or the small silver one a dime?

What's a dime?

You may want to distribute ziplock bags of coins to all your first graders and take some time to review money before you start posing the problems below. Have children practice paying for one cookie, two cookies, then three, and finally four. (Peanut butter cookies cost 4¢ each in our Cookie Store and chocolate chip cookies cost 5¢.) What if they buy one of each kind? Two? What if they don't have enough pennies to make a purchase? Can they think of ways to incorporate nickels and dimes?

If your first graders have studied money and place value counting in previous months, you'll find that many will work in fives and tens before too long. They may not be able to help one another as effectively as before, which may indicate that their own understandings are a bit too delicate to nurture classmates.

Second grade teachers, if you've done some or all of the other themes in this book, you might consider typing some of the problems below on half sheets and giving your students a chance to work independently before you discuss them as a group. By late spring, we found many of our second graders a bit impatient with group work. They seemed happy to have the opportunity to try their own wings.

We did two or three of the easier problems together, and set the rest out in typed form (one problem per half sheet of paper). We encouraged children to select problems of their own choosing, and made various manipulatives available, including the Baker's Dough cookies, the storyboards, coins (quarters, dimes, nickels, and pennies), tiles, Unifix cubes, base ten blocks, and calculators. We asked our students to present their thinking in drawings, numbers, and/or words—an answer alone was not enough.

When everyone had tried at least a few of the problems, we copied an assortment of their solutions onto overheads to share various strategies with the whole class. Not every child had been able to solve every problem, but they celebrated everyone's efforts and learned from one another's endeavors.

Addition

● A young boy brought nine cents to the cookie store. What could he buy? Would he get any change?

Addition / Multiplication

● A Girl Scout bought two chocolate chip cookies and two peanut butter cookies to eat. How much did she have to pay?

● A college student came and bought four chocolate chip cookies. How much did she have to pay?

● A small boy bought two chocolate chip cookies and four peanut butter cookies. How much did he have to pay?

✪ A girl bought nine sugar cookies. How much did she have to pay?

✪ A man bought fourteen chocolate chip cookies. How much did they cost altogether?

Division

✪ A man came in and spent 29¢ on cookies. He left without any change. What could he have bought?

Mixed Operations

● A teacher stopped in to buy some cookies. She gave the clerk a quarter and got a nickel back. What could she have bought?

✪ The man wanted seven peanut butter cookies. He gave the clerk two quarters. How much change should he get?

Creating Story Problems

Even though your students may have created quite a number of story problems by now, we recommend you continue to present problem models for children to examine, solve, and refer to in their own work, because this is only the second time money has come into play in any of the themes. The models you present will give some youngsters an opportunity to challenge their classmates with very open-ended or complex problems, while giving others permission to work at an easier level.

Even this late in the year, we found that most of our children designed problems at their own mathematical comfort level. Some stuck very closely to the models we offered, while others began to take off in new directions. Matthew, a first grader, posed a problem that involved totaling the cost for one chocolate chip cookie at 5¢ and one peanut butter cookie at 4¢. Second grader Sara increased the quantities, the prices, and threw in two different operations:

A girl came in and asked for 9 snickerdoodles and 9 animal cookies to share with her 9 friends, including her. (The snickerdoodles cost 9¢ each and the animal cookies cost 10¢ each.) How much money did she have to pay and how many cookies did each person get?

You will need...

• Buying & Selling problem models, Blacklines B133-B138 and B141-B143
• a variety of problem-solving tools, including ziplock bags of change ((4 dimes, 4 nickels, 15 pennies per bag for first graders; 4 dimes, 4 nickels, 30 pennies, 2 quarters per bag for second graders), Unifix cubes, scratch paper and pencils, and calculators

Begin by asking children to examine the picture portion of one of your problem models. Can they figure out what the problem is by looking at the picture alone? Show them the story problem on the flap. Does the story help to clarify the problem to be solved? Once they've determined what the problem is, ask them to work toward a solution, either mentally or by using any of the tools listed above. Continue in this fashion until you've worked your way through the entire collection of problem models.

THEME 5: THE COOKIE STORE

BUYING AND SELLING COOKIES PROBLEM MODELS

To make copies of these problem models for use in your own classroom, see Blacklines B133-B138 and B141-B143.

Problem Model 6

The grandmother had five grandchildren. She wanted to buy enough cookies that each one would get three to eat. How many should she buy?

Problem Model 7

The clerk took a phone order for three peanut butter cookies and two chocolate chip cookies. How much did the order cost?

167

BUYING & SELLING PROBLEM MODELS (CONT.)

Problem Model 8

Three boys bought a dozen chocolate chip cookies. Each boy wanted to eat his "fair share". How many cookies did each one get?

Problem Model 9

The small girl has 20¢ to spend. What can she buy?

BUYING & SELLING PROBLEM MODELS (CONT.)

**Problem
Model 10**

The boy spent 23¢. He chose some chocolate chip cookies and some peanut butter cookies. How many of each kind did he buy?

Crafting Story Problems

You will need...

- 9" x 12" white, manila or light pastel construction paper, 1 sheet per student
- 4½" x 12" matching paper for story flaps, 1 per student
- 3" x 9" strips of manila paper from which to cut cookies
- assorted cut pieces of construction paper for children to make store clerks and shoppers
- craft "mini curls" fake hair, (optional)
- precut display counters, Blackline B147 (You might want to run these on tan or brown paper.)
- white construction paper in various sizes to make "talking bubbles" for question marks, words, and numbers that signal the problems to be solved
- precut mini-trays, Blackline B149
- precut Cookie Store signs, Blackline B146
- precut Cookie Sale signs, Blackline B146
- crayons, marking pens, scotch tape, and glue to share
- scissors
- writing paper and pencils

Note: Because there is no storyboard associated with this part of the Cookie Store theme, children must create their story problems from scratch, using your problem models for reference.

Once all your problem models have been examined and solved, display them where children can easily refer to each kind as they create their own problems for others to solve. For further details about helping students produce their own story problems, please see the "Crafting Story Problems" section earlier in this chapter (pages 157-159).

Solving Student Problems

You will need...

- selected student problems
- half sheets of ditto paper *or* 8" x 14" mimeo paper folded into quarters for each student
- pencils with erasers
- chalkboards to serve as hard writing surfaces if you're able to gather your children into a group meeting area on the rug
- tiles, Unifix cubes, coins (pennies, nickels, dimes for first graders; you might want to include quarters for second graders), and calculators in an area easily accessible to children

additional materials for second graders:

- base ten pieces, if student problems involve very large numbers
- typed half sheet copies of student story problems (or reduced copies of entire picture problems with story flaps showing) set out so children can select problems they will try to solve independently after the first whole-group sharing session

Once children have completed their own story problems, choose four or five of the more interesting, unique, or challenging student stories for presentation to the group. You might also select a problem that needs reworking in some way. If tactfully handled, children can learn a great deal from errors. Gather your students in a central location, if possible, and distribute paper, pencils, and chalkboards for writing surfaces. Keep other problem-solving materials within easy reach and let the sharing begin.

First Grade Teacher: What do you notice about Brandon's problem?

Children: It looks like the boy is buying some cookies. One peanut butter and two chocolate chip. The store person is trying to figure out how much to charge him. It's four cents and ten cents. That's fourteen cents! Show us his story part. Is that what he wants us to figure out?

The boy had 14¢. How much could he buy?

Children: He sort of gave us the answer in his picture. We don't have to figure it out.

Teacher: What do you mean?

Children: Well, the picture shows the store guy trying to figure out how much to charge for the cookies. And the boy already has a bubble showing he's buying one peanut butter cookie and two chocolate chip cookies. But the story says it a different way. It tells us he has fourteen cents and he's trying to figure out what to buy.

Teacher: Could you help Brandon think of a way to write his story problem so it would match his picture?

Melissa: He could say, "The boy bought one peanut butter cookie and two chocolate chip cookies. How much will it cost?"

Brandon: Can I fix it? That's what I meant.

Teacher: Sure, Brandon. Let's look at Michael's picture. What do you notice?

Children: There's a store person and lots of cookies in the display case. There's a boy shopping for cookies. Is that some money he's holding? We need to read the story part.

He came to the cookie store. He had 25¢. He didn't know what to buy—chocolate chip cookies or peanut butter cookies. He was confused. What do you think he could buy?

Children: Wow! That's a good problem. It's a hard problem!

Teacher: You have paper and pencil. I'd like you to write your own name at the top of the first box and Mike's name at the bottom of that box. Please show me your thinking in pictures, words, or numbers as you figure it out. Be sure to check with your neighbors to see if anyone needs help or has a suggestion that might help you.

Here are some late spring first grade samples of solutions to Michael's problem.

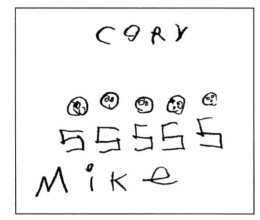

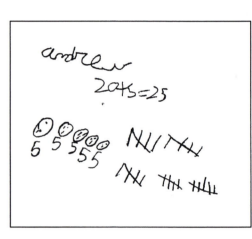

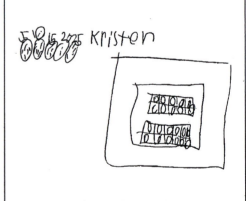

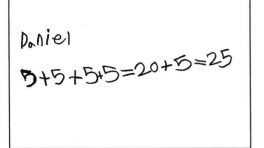

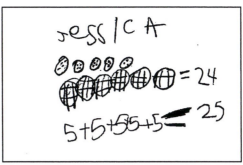

Most children concluded that the boy could buy five chocolate chip cookies at 5¢ each, although Melissa noticed that it was also possible to buy four chocolate chip cookies and one peanut butter cookie for 24¢, and Jessica showed two different solutions: five chocolate chip cookies for 25¢ or six peanut butter cookies for 24¢.

Fewer first graders than second graders were inclined to express their thinking in written words, but they used diagrams, illustrations, and numbers quite effectively. Though not every child was successful, these samples were representative of 85% of the class responses.

We copied a number of student solutions onto overhead transparencies for class discussion and saved children's work (story problems and solutions to other children's problems) for assessment purposes as well.

These were the last story problems our children wrote and solved for the year. When we looked back at their early efforts in September and October, we were surprised and pleased at how far they'd come. The degree and rate of growth each child experienced was different, to be sure. In the end, the skills of these first and second graders ranged from proficiency with beginning addition and subtraction to fair ability with sharing, grouping, partitioning, and mixed operations. The thread common to all was a joy and confidence in solving and posing challenging problems.

III: Graphing Cookie Sales

You will need...

• overhead(s) of Daily Cookie Sales Graph(s), Blacklines B150-B152

• Vis-á-Vis pens, in several different colors, if possible

• an overhead calculator, if you have one

• student calculators to share

• Daily Cookie Sales graphs you plan to use, 1 copy of each per student, Blacklines B150-B152

In this section, you will find three graphing problems, posed at increasing levels of difficulty. The first problem asks children to chart daily sales of giant chocolate chip cookies. We've provided the sales figures and structured the graph in such a way that children need only color in one box per cookie. The challenge lies in comparing quantities sold each day and figuring out total sales for the week.

The second problem also asks children to chart daily sales, but does not provide enough boxes to accommodate the specified quantities. Children must figure out how to construct the graph before they compare and total the sales figures (see page 178).

The third problem asks students to make a double-entry graph, showing daily sales of each type of cookie. Once again, we've provided the sales figures but left it to the children to make some decisions about how to graph them (see page 180).

As you introduce the idea of showing daily cookie sales in graph form, think about your own children. Have you done class graphs throughout the year? Did your children do a Daily Teddy Bear Sales Graph? What level of difficulty would be most appropriate? Would it work in your class to let children choose the level of challenge they'd like to try among the graphing choices?

Display a transparency of the first Daily Cookie Sales Graph on the overhead and discuss it with your class.

Daily Cookie Sales — Graph No. 1

On Monday, the cookie store sold 5 giant chocolate chip cookies. On Tuesday, 7 were sold. On Wednesday, 8 were sold and on Thursday, they sold 3. 10 were sold on Friday and 11 were sold on Saturday.

Show the sales for each day on the grid below:

Mon.												
Tues.												
Wed.												
Thurs.												
Fri.												
Sat.												

On which day were the fewest cookies sold? _____

On which day were the most cookies sold? _____

Were more cookies sold Monday or Tuesday? _____

How many more? _____

How many cookies were sold altogether that week? _____

174

Teacher: Let's read the top portion of the graphing sheet on the overhead together and see if we can figure out what to do.

Children: It's like some of the other graphs we've made. We have to color it in. Are there enough boxes? Do we color one in for every cookie they sold? Could we draw a round cookie in each box?

Teacher: You could color a box for each cookie or draw a cookie in each box.

Children: We did that on the the Bear Sales graph, too. I liked doing that one.

Teacher: How about the questions at the bottom? Will you be able to figure out each of those?

Children: It should be easy once we have the cookie part all finished. Can we use the calculators?

Teacher: Of course. How would you go about using them to solve these problems?

Children: Can we fill in the boxes on your sheet so we can see how it all looks? Then we can use the calculators. I love playing with them. Me, too!

Teacher: That sounds like a good idea. What do you want me to do first?

Children: Draw cookies for Monday. They sold five. Draw five cookies. Make some dots for the chocolate chips.

Continue following children's directions until you've filled in cookies or colored in enough boxes to indicate specified cookie sales for Monday through Thursday.

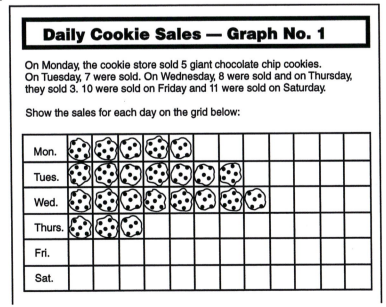

Daily Cookie Sales — Graph No. 1

On Monday, the cookie store sold 5 giant chocolate chip cookies.
On Tuesday, 7 were sold. On Wednesday, 8 were sold and on Thursday, they sold 3. 10 were sold on Friday and 11 were sold on Saturday.

Show the sales for each day on the grid below:

Teacher: I want to stop here so you'll still have some problems to solve if you choose this graphing paper. How could the calculators help you answer the questions?

Children: We have to read them first. Could you help us read the first one?

Teacher: Sure. It asks, "On which day were the fewest cookies sold?"

Children: Does that mean not very many? Is that like the most less? I think it means hardly any.

Teacher: Good definitions, all of you. You might also think of it as the least.

Children: It's easy then. It was three. Thursday. They only sold three that day. We don't need the calculators for that.

Kristen: I can read the next question. It says, "On which day were the most sold?"

Children: Wednesday. They sold eight.

Teacher: That's true if we're only looking at these four days of sales. Would that be true for the whole week?

Alexis: No, because it says they sold eleven Saturday and ten on Friday. That's more than Wednesday.

Children: Let's do the next one. I want to use the calculators. Me too.

Michael: It says "Were more cookies sold on Monday or Tuesday?" We don't need them for that answer.

Children: Tuesday. Seven on Tuesday!

Rutta: But the next question says "How many more?

Children: Two more! We didn't need the calculators. We just can see it.

Teacher: Suppose you did want to figure it out with the calculator? What would you do?

Children: We could push in a five. Yeah! And a seven. Oh, oh! I got 57! Me too. Not me, I got twelve. I did a plus. Not me, I got so many numbers in this window, I don't even know what it says.

Andrew: Somehow it's got to end up with two. You can see it was two more. Maybe you can't do it on the calculator.

Teacher: What do you think?

Eilbert: I've got it! I got two.

Children: How? What did you do?

Eilbert: I punched seven—then the take away—then five. It kept showing five in the window till I remembered to push the equals button.

Teacher: Why do you think that worked?

Children: Because seven take away five equals two. But we're supposed to figure out how many more. I thought you always push plus for more, but I keep getting twelve. I do too.

Jessica: You keep telling us to figure out the difference. Is that the same as the take away sign?

Teacher: It's quite confusing, isn't it? The numbers we get on the calculator don't always seem to help. But you understood that the answer on the calculator wasn't always a reasonable answer, so you kept trying other things. Let's try one more. Can you figure out how many more cookies were sold on Wednesday than on Monday?

The discussion above was very typical of our first and second graders. Finding the difference between two quantities was never easy except on a graph and even then, their understanding of the term "fewer than" was tenuous at best.

Symbolizing the process was even more difficult, so it was interesting to watch them struggle to get the calculator to show the answer they already knew to be correct. So great was their motivation to use the calculator, though, that it served as a tool to teach standard notation of various operations from time to time. We were always impressed, too, at the kind of discussion that went on about when and how to use calculators. Even some of the youngest children seemed to realize that sometimes a visual or mental solution was faster, or easier, or more reliable.

Teacher: I think you've done some mighty fine investigating and I'm extremely proud of you. The best part is that you weren't willing to accept answers that didn't make sense. Let's look at the last question on the page. How would you use the calculators to solve that question?

Children: I think you just keep putting in numbers and pushing plus. Me too. Let's try it.

Teacher: Let's see if we can figure it out for just the days that we've filled in so far for the cookie sales.

Children: I think it's twenty-one. No, it's twenty-three. I got that too. Not me. I got five thousand, seven hundred and eighty-three. You forgot to push plus. I pushed plus and I got 3. You forgot to push equals. Let's count up the cookies and see what it's supposed to be.

Teacher: You surely could count, but does anyone have a faster way to figure it out?

Alyssa: I see four fives and three—twenty-three! (She comes to the overhead and circles groups of five.)

Teacher: Great problem solving! Any other ways?

Mike: I went five, six, seven, eight, nine, ten, eleven, twelve, thirteen, fourteen, fifteen, sixteen, seventeen, eighteen, nineteen, twenty, twenty-one, twenty-two, twenty-three.

Teacher: Another good way. Who has a different way?

Daniel: I looked at it up and down. I went four plus four is eight and then four more is twelve...three more is fifteen and three more is eighteen and two more is twenty, then twenty-two, twenty-three.

Children: So everybody who got twenty-three on the calculator must have pushed the right buttons! I did. So did I. I think I just forgot one of the numbers because I got twenty. Not me, I got all messed up.

The next day, display the second Daily Cookie Sales Graph on the overhead. This graph offers a different sort of challenge, in that there are not enough boxes to use one per cookie.

Daily Cookie Sales — Graph No. 2

The cookie store owner was eager to figure out how many sugar cookies the store had sold altogether during the week. She found out they had sold 3 dozen on Monday, 2 dozen on Tuesday, 5 dozen on Wednesday, 4 dozen on Thursday, and 7 dozen on Friday.

Show the sales for each day on the grid below:

On which day were the fewest sugar cookies sold? _____

On which day were the most sugar cookies sold? _____

How many sugar cookies (*not dozens*) did the store sell on Monday? _____

How many sugar cookies (*not dozens*) did the store sell on Friday? _____

How many cookies did the store sell altogether, Monday through Friday? _____

Teacher: Here's a graphing sheet that's a bit more difficult. You'll probably want to use your calculators to help figure out the questions on the bottom once you've completed the graph.

Children: I want to do that one. But there aren't enough boxes. Yeah, three dozen...that's a lot of cookies. There aren't enough boxes.

Teacher: That's an interesting problem. What could you do about it?

Johnny: We could tape a bunch of sheets together.

Teacher: That's a possibility. How many sheets would you need to tape together?

Children: 3 dozen, hmmm...that's twelve and twelve, and twelve more. That's a real lot. Twelve and twelve is twenty-four!

Teacher: How many boxes are there across this sheet?

Faith: Nine—I was counting them.

JoDell: But we'll need one in each row to put the name of the day in—we'll only have eight to use.

Scottie: Wow, we'd really have to tape lots of sheets together.

Teacher: Is there anything else you could do?

Kaylyn: I know! Remember in the bear graph, lots of us used one box for five bears? We could do that again.

Timmy: We could use one box for a dozen. That would be easy. Then we'd only need to color in three boxes for Monday.

Ryan: Yeah, and two for Tuesday, and five for Wednesday!

Breanna: Then you'd have to use the calculators to figure out those questions. That's a lot of cookies.

The third Daily Cookie Sales Graph (see following page) is a second grade challenge. Not only does it involve sales figures for both chocolate chip and peanut butter cookies; it also asks children to calculate the amount of money made on two different days. This is a scaled down version of our original worksheet, which was too hard for even the most capable students. We think it poses some interesting problems within reach of many seven- and eight-year-olds.

Teacher: The third graphing sheet is incredibly challenging. Look it over and see if any of you would be willing to try it. What do you notice?

Children: The numbers talk about how many chocolate chip and how many sugar cookies they sold each day. How are we going to do that? Oh, I see—there are two rows for each day. We can make each row be for a different kind of cookie—like the top row for sugar cookies and the bottom row for chocolate chip. We'll have to show it in dozens though, there aren't enough boxes for cookies.

Teacher: This is a challenge you don't have to take on unless you choose. The problems at the bottom of the sheet are particularly interesting.

Children: I want to try it. Me too!

Daily Cookie Sales — Graph No. 3

On Monday, the cookie store sold 3 dozen chocolate chip cookies and 2 dozen peanut butter cookies. On Tuesday, they sold 4 dozen chocolate chip cookies and 3 dozen peanut butter cookies. On Wednesday, they sold 2 dozen chocolate chip cookies and 1 dozen peanut butter cookies. On Thursday, they sold 5 dozen chocolate chip cookies and 2 dozen peanut butter cookies. On Friday, they sold 4 dozen chocolate chip cookies and 3 dozen peanut butter cookies.

Show the sales for each day on the grid below:

On which day were the fewest cookies sold?_____ The most?_____

How many peanut butter cookies (*not dozens*) were sold Wednesday?_____

On Wednesday, how much money did the store make by selling peanut butter cookies at 4¢ each?_____

How many chocolate chip cookies (*not dozens*) were sold Monday?_____

On Wednesday, how much money did the store make by selling chocolate chip cookies at 5¢ each?_____

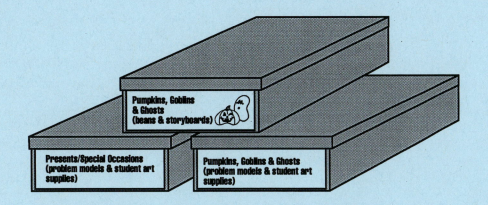

Preparation
of Materials

Preparation of Materials

The materials needed to implement these units include five storyboxes, each containing a class set of storyboards and about three hundred fifty to four hundred fifty teacher-produced counters (for a class of thirty), overheads of the storyboards, problem models, and such basic tools as Unifix cubes and calculators.

While the preparation of these materials will require some work beforehand, we've included many blacklines to make your life easier, as well as a set of instructions which we hope will make you chuckle. You can simply run copies of **Storyboards** and **Problem Models** for each theme. With some coloring, door taping, and story problem flap gluing and taping, they'll be ready. **Overheads** for each unit can be easily prepared. **Storybox counters** will require the most time because three of the storyboxes call for spray-painted lima beans with hand-drawn faces. (The counters for Presents and Cookies take less time). You'll also need to gather classroom arts and crafts supplies for the children to use when they create their own story problems for each theme.

Storybox Counters

Punchout carboard "lima bean" characters, gifts, and cookies can now be ordered from MLC Materials (address and phone number on page 191). They're colored and the faces are all drawn for you! A first and second grade set (adequate for a class of 30 pupils) is $75. Sets for individual themes may be purchased separately.

If you want to make the counters yourself, read on. Painting lima beans does take some time. First you have to shop for the right colors. After the first coat or two of spray paint, you have to get the blooming things turned over so you can spray the other side. Then you have to pretend to be a real artist and draw a face on each of the beans, and finally spray on a coat of clear gloss varnish so those charming features will endure longer. You'll find yourself dreaming about beans! Worse yet, your fabulous creations won't last forever. Three years of looking good and then the wear begins to show if your children are using them often.

But those of you who enjoy crafts will probably find most of this very satisfying—until you begin to glue ears on the teddy bears. This task may call for a party whereby guests can only collect refreshments after gluing twenty or more pairs of ears on your bean bears; we like to tell them it's community service. We're proposing that you have your students make their own cookies to save you that grief, but if you're totally compulsive about getting it all done ahead of time, we'll understand.

We'll try to make it as easy as we can in our directions below; if you truly hate this kind of work, we suggest you might organize an assembly line of parent volunteers or sixth graders to help, or even call on relatives or friends who owe you a favor. If you have fellow teachers who will be doing this also, it's much cheaper if you buy paints to share. We hope after all your work, you'll believe as we do, that it was absolutely worth it!

LIMA BEANS

Buy large (not baby) dry lima beans. If your grocery store offers beans in more than one grade, buy the more expensive packages—you'll almost always have fewer broken beans to throw away. We find one pound of lima beans gives us about 375–400 unbroken beans to paint. To make the counters for all three themes that require beans, you'll need four pounds if you have twenty to twenty-four children in your class. If you have more students, buy five pounds.

SPRAY PAINTING TIPS

Purchase fast drying gloss or matte finish spray paint for each color recommended (see below). We find WalMart, K Mart, Target, Sears, Payless Drugs, Venture, hardware stores, paint stores, or home improvement stores to be good sources. One can of spray paint (not the small craft cans) will usually cover about three pounds of beans, front and back.

Spread out more newspaper than you think you'll need and spray away from buildings, cars, etc., in order to keep your good reputation intact. (The paint does drift a bit.) We find it best to spray a light coat, let it dry a few minutes and then spray again for good coverage. It dries more thoroughly than if you spray on one heavy coat.

These beans should be painted on both sides, but turning them over can be a real pain. The easiest way is to have two identical cookie sheets protected by foil or two identical sheets of heavy cardboard available. Spread the lima beans out flat on one sheet and spray them lightly (usually two coats). When dry, place the extra sheet over the painted beans and hold the two sheets tightly while you flip them over. If you can hold on tightly enough, most of the beans should be turned over when you remove the top sheet.

The other way is to just let the first coats of paint dry, then lightly toss handfuls of beans and hope at least half of them come down with the un-painted-side up. You'll have to hand turn those that don't. Keep a mint julep, espresso coffee, or your favorite soft drink nearby.

We like to leave painted (and dried) beans in an open container for a day or two so the paint fumes diminish before we draw on them.

DRAWING FACES ON BEANS

Use ultra-fine Sanford Sharpie pens (available by the dozen at discount office/business supply places). We keep two or three pens beside us along with a scratch pad. After drawing with a pen for a few minutes, we scribble on a scratch pad and then replace the cap. (There's a bit of paint residue on the beans that can clog the tips, so it's important to clean them off on paper fairly often.) We trade pens frequently to keep them from drying out. Place finished beans on a sheet of cardboard for easy varnishing.

When all the faces have been drawn, place your cardboard tray of beans on newspaper and spray a coat of inexpensive clear gloss fast-drying varnish to the face side. The varnish keeps little fingers from rubbing off those incredible details you drew. Don't leave the beans outside overnight. Climate changes and heavy moisture can cause deterioration.

SPRAY PAINT COLOR NEEDS AND QUANTITIES OF BEANS

Note: The quantities suggested below are based on a class of 30.

School Bus Kids
1 can tan spray paint
1 can brown spray paint
1 can peach spray paint (or unpainted white beans)
    Spray 130 or more beans (about 1 cup) per color. After the beans are dried and aired, start drawing. You'll want to end up with a total of thirteen kid beans for each student.

Face Samples:

(If you're totally compulsive, use a Q-tip or small paint brush with a bit of diluted red-orange paint to blush cheeks onto the bean faces before you apply the final varnish coat. We pick up a touch of paint, blot our Q-tip or brush on a paper towel and then "blush" about ten beans before picking up more paint. The drier the paint brush, the better! We find diluted acrylic paints work well.)

Pumpkins, Goblins, and Ghosts
1 can green spray paint
1 can orange spray paint
add unpainted white beans for ghosts
    Spray 240 or more beans (about 1¾ cups) per color and leave about 240 white. You'll want to end up with eight or more of each character for each student. Once the paint has dried and aired, start drawing simple faces.

Face Samples:

pumpkins   goblins   ghosts

Night Critters
(In case you aren't choosing to do Pumpkins, Goblins, and Ghosts)
1 can green spray paint
1 can magenta spray paint

Spray 240 or more beans (about 1 ³/₄ cups) per color. After the beans are dried and aired, start drawing. You'll want to end up with eight or more of each color for each student.

Face Samples:

Teddy Bears
1 can medium brown spray paint (not dark—you want your faces to show)

Spray 240 or more beans (about 1³/₄ cups) brown and leave about 1³/₄ cups white. After the beans have dried and aired, start drawing. You'll want to end up with eight or more of each color for each student. Once the beans are dry, draw on the faces.

There are three ways to deal with ears. The easiest is to simply draw them right on the bear as pictured below. Another way is to cut ears from felt, which is economical but horrendously time-consuming.

The cutest and quickest way (if you remember to hold a party and coerce your friends into helping) is to buy packages of small pom poms from a craft or fabric store in white and brown. It will cost a bundle—but you'll love them when you get over hating the work they involve. Use Tacky glue (we like the kind in the brown bottle). Squeeze out a small puddle at a time and use a toothpick to put on two generous globs per bean. (We put glue on ten or more beans at a time and then go back and set the ears into place.) We also keep a small bottle of tacky glue at school to repair any ears that might fall off in use.

Face Samples:

drawn ears   felt ears   pom pom ears

Presents (Christmas or Special Occasion)
Purchase or gather several Christmas or special occasion sheets of gift wrap with tiny designs, as well as one small can of spray adhesive (available in photo supply stores, hardware stores, and many craft stores). You'll also need two large sheets of posterboard cut into three or four pieces about 14" x 20".

Cut three or four sheets of gift wrap to manageable size (no more than 12" x 18").

Spread out newspaper to cover your **outside** working area—this spray also drifts. These fumes will send you and your loved ones into Lala Land if you don't work outside. Cover one of your posterboard sheets with adhesive spray and quickly spread a sheet of gift wrap over it. Continue with your other sheets of gift wrap until all are adhered to posterboard.

When the fumes have gone away, cut the gift wrap into small present shapes on your paper cutter—if you haven't received one for an anniversary, Christmas present or birthday gift by now, it's time! Cut presents in sizes from ½" x 1" to 1½" x 1½" so they will fit the storyboards easily. You won't need to cut up more than half of each piece for now. Save the rest to cut when children create their own story problems. You want to end up with 12 or more presents for each student to use for solving problems. These will be non-consumable, and go back into your Presents story box each year. You'll also want to cut at least 12 per child for students to consume when they create their own story problems.

Cookies (Baker's Dough)

The easiest way to handle the cookies is to have each of your students make two dozen in class. Ask a parent volunteer to take them home and bake them. Those of you who live in humid climates will definitely want to do it this way. Baker's Dough tends to deteriorate in high humidity over time.

Student-Prepared Baker's Dough Cookies—yield: 24 tiny cookies: 12 "chocolate chip" and 12 "peanut butter". (See Blackline B153 to run copies of the student recipe.)

Mix:
   8 Tablespoons of white flour
   2 Tablespooons plus 2 teaspoons of salt
Add:
   2 Tablespooons plus 2 teaspoons of water

Stir until thoroughly mixed. If the mixture seems a little too dry, add a few drops of water. If it is too sticky, add a little bit of flour.

Knead for several minutes until the entire ball feels smooth and elastic. Break off half of it and form it into twelve "peanut butter" cookies. Your cookies shouldn't be much bigger than nickels. Use a fork to add a criss cross to the top of each cookie before you bake.

Use the other half to form twelve "chocolate chip" cookies. After you bake them, dot on brown tempera paint with a Q-tip for chocolate chips.

Place all of your cookies on a piece of foil (with your name on it) to be baked at 275° for an hour, or until hard and nicely browned.

Clean up your entire mess to stay in the good graces of your teacher!

186

Teacher or Parent Volunteer-Prepared Baker's Dough Cookies (You'll probably need to make two or three batches of the recipe below depending upon your class size. You want to have 24 cookies per student—12 "chocolate chip" and 12 "peanut butter")

Mix:

4 cups white flour

1 cup salt

Add:

1½ cups water

Stir until thoroughly mixed. If the mixture seems a little too dry, add water bit by bit until the dough holds together without being too sticky. (If it should end up feeling sticky anyway, pour a layer of flour onto your bread board or counter top and as you begin to knead the dough, the extra flour will solve the problem.)

Knead for several minutes until the entire ball feels smooth and elastic. Break off about a fourth of the ball at a time and use a rolling pin to roll it to about ¼" thickness.

Find a pill bottle plastic lid (or coin tube lid) about the size of a nickel and cut zillions of cookies. This will cease to be fun after the first hundred—the kids would have had a great time doing it themselves!

Use a fork on half of the cookies to form criss cross marks like those on real peanut butter cookies.

Bake the cookies at 275° for about an hour or until they feel firm to the touch.

Once the cookies are cooled, or another day when you're not so fed up with this whole mess, add "chocolate chips" to the half that isn't peanut butter. We used a brown "slick" pen like those used to decorate T-shirts and sweat shirts to add "chips". You can buy several different brands in most craft or fabric stores. (Be sure to ask someone for the kind that dries—not the puff-type that stays soft.) Adding chips goes quickly and allows you to forget how you felt about these cookies the day before. You can also use a brown marking pen or even pour out a bit of brown tempera on a margarine lid and dot on chips with a Q-tip.

Storage Boxes

We use ten Standard Boxes (which can be ordered from MLC Materials, P.O. Box 3226, Salem, OR, phone 503-370-8130), two for each theme. One is used to house the beans and storyboards, the other to hold our Problem Models and the arts and crafts materials students will need to create their own problems. We cover the tops and bottoms of our boxes with Contact paper so they will last a very long time. You'll find Storybox Labels on Blackline B4.

Storyboards

Before you begin each theme, locate the storyboards in the blacklines and run copies for each student. You'll notice that School Bus Kids and Presents have two storyboards each. You'll need to run a copy of each per student. The other themes each have only one storyboard.

Each storyboard (except the fireplace board for Presents) needs a secret door cut from construction paper. Attach each door with scotch tape on one side so it opens easily. The door for Cookies will be taped at the bottom of the oven.

Once these are finished, store them in a prepared standard size box along with the counters for that theme.

School Bus Kids

Tape a 2" x 3" piece of colored construction paper over each house door. Make two boards—one arriving and one departing board—for each student. It will be easier to have children get hold of the same board if you use a different color door on the arriving set than on the departing set.

Pumpkins, Goblins, and Ghosts

Cut a black construction paper door to tape over the door on each haunted house.

Night Critters

Cut a construction paper door to fit over the closet door in each bedroom.

Presents

Tape a 3" x 6" construction paper door to the right of each Christmas tree or table to serve as the closet door. (There is no secret door for the fireplace board.)

Teddy Bear Store

Tape a 2" x 2¾" construction paper door over the opening on each teddy bear truck.

Cookie Store

Tape a 3½" x 5" white construction paper door over the oven door space on each stove.

Problem Models

Locate the problem models for each theme in the blacklines and run one copy of each on white cardstock. (We chose cardstock because we wanted them to be more durable than paper.) These can be prepared a few days prior to implementation of each new theme or you could do them all beforehand. They can be left black and white, or colored if you have time and want to do so. You'll note that many of them need corresponding doors. Locate the doors by problem number to add where needed. Tape each door in place with "hinges" of scotch tape.

School Bus Kids

Locate the corresponding doors for Problem Models 1, 3, 4, and 5. Make a copy of each door to cut and tape over the corresponding house doorway.

Locate the door panel for Problem Model 6 and tape it to cover the right side of the picture portion.

Pumpkins, Goblins, and Ghosts (Secret Door Patterns)

Locate the two Secret Door Linear Pattern Problem Models in the blacklines. Make a copy of each. Cut a small construction paper "secret door" to tape at the top of each so it forms a lift-up door over a piece of the pattern. Place one of the doors at the beginning of one pattern and the other in the middle of the second pattern.

Locate the 3 x 3, 4 x 4, and 5 x 5 grid patterns in the blacklines. Cut construction paper "lift-up secret doors" to tape over the center square of the pattern on the 3 x 3, three or four squares on the 4 x 4, and four or five squares on the 5 x 5. You want enough of the pattern showing on each that the children can gather adequate information from what they see to figure out what's hidden. Be sure your doors are taped so they will lift!

Pumpkins, Goblins and Ghosts (Whole Number Operations)

Locate the doors for Problem Models 2 and 3. Make a cardstock copy; cut and tape each door over the corresponding problem's haunted house doorway.

Locate the door panels for Problem Models 5, 6, 7, and 8.

Problem Model 5: Tape the door panel to cover the left side of the picture portion.

Problem Model 6: Tape the door panel to cover the right side of the picture portion.

Problem Model 7: Tape the door panel to cover the left side of the picture portion.

Problem Model 8: Tape the door panel to cover the right side of the picture portion.

Night Critters

Locate the doors for Problem Models. Make a cardstock copy of the closet doors, then cut and tape each one over the corresponding problem model doorway.

Christmas Presents

Locate the doors for Problem Models 1, 4, 5, and 8. Make a cardstock copy to cut and tape over the corresponding problem model closet doorways. (The fireplace boards don't have any secret doors.)

Special Occasion Presents

Locate the doors for Problems Models 1, 4, 5, 6, 8, and 9. Make a cardstock copy to cut apart and tape over the corresponding problem model closet doors.

The Teddy Bear Store

Locate the doors for Problems 1, 2, 3, 4, 5, 6, 7, and 8. Make cardstock copies of each. Cut and tape over the corresponding problem model truck doors or store shelves as needed.

The Cookie Store

Locate the page of doors for Problem Models 1, 2, 3, 4, and 5. Make a cardstock copy of the doors to cut and tape to the corresponding problems.

Problem Model Story Flaps

Locate the Story Flaps for each theme. Run on white cardstock and cut apart. Use scotch tape hinges to attach each completed story problem flap to the bottom of the corresponding problem model picture.

Overheads

If you are accustomed to using an overhead in your classroom, copy each of the storyboards onto an overhead transparency by using either your school thermofax machine or blackline copier. Locate the blackline "Storybox Characters for Overheads" and create a transparency to cut and color. We find Sanford Sharpies work well to color transparencies. You'll have to experiment with other permanent pens to see which will adhere.

General Materials

Along with the storyboards and counters, students use Unifix cubes, 1" square plastic or ceramic tiles, Base Ten Counting Pieces, and calculators to help solve teacher- and student-posed story problems. These materials can be ordered from many different math and early childhood supply catalogues but we find The Math Learning Center has both excellent prices and service.

The address is:
  MLC Materials
  P. O. Box 3226
  Salem, Oregon 97302
  Phone 503-370-8130

Though we find that the Base Ten Counting Pieces produced by The Math Learning Center are excellent, any base ten counting blocks could be used. You will want to provide several sets.

We also use ziplock bags of real coins when children are working on the Cookie Store problems. We furnish the money ourselves in our own classrooms but know several teachers who have asked children to donate pennies, nickels, dimes, and quarters for class use over the year.

Arts & Crafts Supplies

To create their own story problems for each theme, students use typical classroom arts and crafts supplies. These include:

• scissors

• glue

• colored construction paper

• marking pens

• crayons

• glitter

We purchase:

• a dozen or more ultra-fine Sanford Sharpies for the children to use when drawing faces on their construction paper beans (NEVER use near glue).

• "mini-curl" craft hair to add to the people in the student-created problems.

We precut (or ask parents to precut):

• lima-bean shaped construction paper beans in appropriate colors for the children to use when adding the characters to their story problems (We've included a blackline of the bean shapes in case you want to staple four sheets of appropriately colored construction paper beneath a copy of the bean shapes to send out to a parent—community service! Four sheets should get you through most themes depending upon your class size.) If you're cutting the paper beans freehand, which we find to be fairly quick, cut four 9" x 12" sheets of each needed color. We use a small, sharp pair of scissors—it's easier on our fingers and faster.

• Don't forget to cut up your remaining gift wrap/posterboard for the children to use in crafting their own presents story problems.

Feely Box

 You will need a stretchy adult sock and a plastic pint refrigerator container. Push plastic container down into the toe of the sock. Cut strips of paper on which to write each student's name.

References

Baratta-Lorton, Mary. 1978. *Workjobs II.* Menlo Park, Calif.: Addison Wesley.

Burk, Donna, Allyn Snider, and Paula Symonds. 1988. *Box It or Bag It Mathematics Resource Guide, Grades 1-2.* Salem, Ore.: Math Learning Center.

Burningham. John. 1971. *Mr. Gumpy's Outing.* New York: Holt.

Burns, Marilyn. 1992. *About Teaching Mathematics, A K-8 Resource.* Portsmouth, N.H.: Heinemann.

California Department of Education. 1992. *Mathematics Framework for California Public Schools, Kindergarten Through Grade Twelve.* Sacramento, Calif.: California Department of Education.

Carle, Eric. 1987. *Rooster's Off to See the World.* Saxonville, Ma.: Picture Book Studio.

Crowe, Robert L. 1986. *Clyde Monster.* New York: Dutton Books.

Gackenback, Dick. 1984. *Harry and the Terrible Whatzit.* Burlington, Ma.: Houghton Mifflin.

Gardner, Howard. 1983. *Frames of Mind.* New York: Basic Books.

Hawkins, Colin and Jacqui. 1988. *How Many Are in This Old Car?* New York: Putnam.

Head, Debby, Libby Pollett, and Michael Arcidiacono. 1991. *Opening Eyes to Mathematics.* Salem, Ore.: Math Learning Center.

Howe, James. 1990. *There's a Monster Under My Bed.* New York: Macmillan.

Kamii, Constance. 1989. *Young Children Continue to Reinvent Arithmetic.* New York: Teachers College Press.

Kamii, Constance. 1985. *Young Children Reinvent Arithmetic.* New York: Teachers College Press.

Mayer, Mercer. 1985. *There's a Nightmare in My Closet.* New York: Dial Books.

Mayer, Mercer. 1987. *What Do You Do With a Kangaroo?* New York: Scholastic.

McQueen, John Troy. 1986. *A World Full of Monsters.* New York: Harper and Row.

Moss, Marissa. 1991. *After-School Monster.* New York: Puffin Books.

National Council of Teachers of Mathematics. 1989. *Curriculum and Evaluation Standards for School Mathematics*. Reston, Va.: National Council of Teachers of Mathematics.

National Council of Teachers of Mathematics. 1991. *Curriculum and Evaluation Standards for School Mathematics Addenda Series, First-Grade Book*. Reston, Va.: National Council of Teachers of Mathematics.

National Council of Teachers of Mathematics. 1992. *Curriculum and Evaluation Standards for School Mathematics Addenda Series, Second-Grade Book*. Reston, Va.: National Council of Teachers of Mathematics.

Rees, Mary. 1988. *Ten in a Bed*. Denver, Colo.: Little.

Skinner, Penny. 1991. *What's Your Problem? Posing and Solving Mathematical Problems, K-2*. Portsmouth, N.H.: Heinemann.

Stoessiger, Rex and Joy Edmunds. 1992. *Natural Learning and Mathematics*. Portsmouth, N.H.: Heinemann.

Von Glasersfeld, Ernst, ed. 1991. *Radical Constructivism in Mathematics Education*. Boston, Mass.: Kluwer Academic Publishers.

Winthrop, Elizabeth. 1987. *Maggie and the Monster*. New York: Holiday House.